PERSPECTIVES ON EARLY CHILDHOOD PSYCHOLOGY AND EDUCATION

SPECIAL FOCUS

Methodological Innovations for Advancing Early Childhood Educational and Psychological Research

Volume 8, Issue 2
Fall 2023

Copyright © 2023
Pace University Press
41 Park Row
15th floor
New York, NY 10038

ISBN: 978-1-935625-86-5
ISSN: 2471-1527

Member

Council of Editors of Learned Journals

PERSPECTIVES on EARLY CHILDHOOD PSYCHOLOGY and EDUCATION

EDITOR
Maria Hernández Finch, *Ball State University*

GUEST EDITOR
Anthony Mangino, *University of Kentucky*

ASSOCIATE EDITORS
Tammy Hughes, *Duquesne University*
Barbara A. Mowder, *Pace University*
Flo Rubinson, *Brooklyn College*
Beth Trammell, *Indiana University East*

EDITORIAL ASSISTANTS
Josephine Bucker
Jessica Otey

EDITORIAL REVIEW BOARD
Vincent C. Alfonso, *Gonzaga University*
Stefano Bagnato, *University of Pittsburgh*
Renee Bergeron, *Consultant*
Zeynep Biringen, *Colorado State University*
Bruce A. Bracken, *College of William & Mary*
Melissa Bray, *University of Connecticut*
Victoria Comerchero, *Touro College*
Gerard Costa, *Montclair State University*
Grace Elizade-Utnick, *City University of New York at Brooklyn College*
Kathryn Fletcher, *Ball State University*
Gilbert Foley, *New York Center for Child Development*
Laurie Ford, *University of British Columbia*
Pamela Guess, *University of Tennessee*
Robin Hojnoski, *Lehigh University*
Anthony Mangino, *University of Kentucky*
Sara McCane-Bowling, *University of Tennessee*
David McIntosh, *Ball State University*
Geraldine Oades-Sese, *Rutgers Robert Wood Johnson Medical School*
Matt Reynolds, *University of Kansas*
Gail Ross, *NY Presbyterian Hospital*
Susan Ruby, *Eastern Washington University*
Mark Sossin, *Pace University*
Esther Stavrou, *Yeshiva University*

Mark Terjesen, *St. John's University*
Lea A. Theodore, *College of William and Mary*
Mary Ward, *Weill Cornell Medical College*
Adriana Wissel, *Gonzaga University*

TABLE OF CONTENTS

Editor's Note vii
Maria Hernández Finch

Introduction to the Special Issue: Methodological Innovations for Advancing Early Childhood Educational and Psychological Research ix
Anthony Mangino, Guest Editor

**SPECIAL FOCUS:
METHODOLOGICAL INNOVATIONS FOR ADVANCING EARLY CHILDHOOD EDUCATIONAL AND PSYCHOLOGICAL RESEARCH**

Early Education Indirect Service Research with Generalization Data: A Systematic Review of Single-Case Design Methodological Rigor 1
Zachary C. LaBrot, Brittany Garza, Tyler Smith, Emily Maxime, and Abigail Lawson

Using Effect Sizes, Confidence Intervals, and the Bayes Factor to Better Understand the t-test, Analysis of Variance, and Regression Results 43
W. Holmes Finch

Using Multilevel Modeling to Understand Nested Data 69
W. Holmes Finch

A Tutorial for Identifying and Comparing Changepoints in Developmental Trajectories 87
W. Holmes Finch

Comparison of Multidimensional Models for Extreme Response Styles 103
W. Holmes Finch and Brian F. French

Latent Transition Analysis: A Statistical Method for Identifying Underlying Subgroups over Time 127
W. Holmes Finch

LIST OF CONTRIBUTORS 151

EDITORIAL POLICY 153

Editor's Note

Maria Hernández Finch

 We are very pleased to offer a series of articles that when taken as a whole offer tutorials for early education researchers interested in providing updated and innovative approaches to analyzing early childhood data. Our Guest Editor, Dr. Anthony Mangino, authored a reflective and thorough introduction to the issue. We welcome submissions of other methodological articles that focus on early childhood research metanalyses, scoping reviews, tutorials with examples, data simulations, and other formats.

Guest Editor's Introduction: Methodological Innovations for Advancing Early Childhood Educational and Psychological Research

Anthony Mangino

"Don't be afraid of statistics, research design is more difficult." This phrase is nearly axiomatic in the training of research methodologists, particularly for those of us in the social sciences. It is well-understood that human subjects research carries with it qualities of uncertainty, stochasticity, philosophical doubt, and to some extent, a willful suspension of disbelief given that the variability within a single individual is often greater than that between any two individuals in a study. In the context of early childhood development and education research, every challenge in both *designing* an effective, informative, valid, and replicable study, and *conducting* sufficiently comprehensive and reasonable analyses is compounded by several factors: The age of the participants, the rapid pace of psychomotor and psychosocial development, and the corresponding need for simultaneously precise, yet adaptable, study designs and data collection methods, among others. Despite these challenges, it is of paramount importance that we continually examine design and analytic methods that enable us to study the rapid and multifaceted development of children throughout their early years of life. The impetus is then on us, the scientists, to continually improve our own domain-specific knowledge base and methodological understanding such that we can succeed in the careful, nuanced examination of developmental phenomena.

The goal of this special issue is to provide you, the inquisitive reader and developmental scientist, with some of the methodological tools to aid in augmenting your analytic capacity. The first manuscript *Early Education Indirect Service Research with Generalization Data* presents a systematic review of single-case study designs (specifically those involving 'real world' contexts), and evaluates the found literature against both the current and historic research design and analysis standards of WhatWorks Clearinghouse. Our second manuscript *Using Effect Sizes, Confidence Intervals, and the Bayes Factor to Better Understand the t-test* details the use of methods alternative to (or that can augment) the traditional significance test; in particular, given the possibility of small samples in early childhood research, such non-significance test-based representations are crucial. The third manuscript, *Using Multilevel Modeling to Understand Nested Data*, bridges the gap between the first and second halves of this special issue by introducing an analytic paradigm useful in both cross-sectional and longitudinal research, namely multilevel modeling. Among the widely available analytic paradigms, multilevel modeling is one of the most flexible, and has been used in a variety of study designs and domains of inquiry.

Expanding upon one specific capability of multilevel modeling, a common thread among some of the latter manuscripts in this special issue is the notion of *time* as a principal independent variable. The next manuscript in this sequence, *A Tutorial for Identifying and Comparing Change Points in Developmental Trajectories*, focuses on change point identification—detecting meaningful and persistent differences in the mean and/or variance of a measure over time—and employs some of the principles of Bayesian data analysis examined in the second manuscript in this special issue. The manuscript *Comparison of Multidimensional Models for Extreme Response Styles* presents an overview of a commonly-observed phenomenon in self-report measures that can substantially reduce the validity, and by extension generalizability, of results in studies involving self-report measures by endorsing an extreme position without a corresponding belief in that position. When considering the inherent uncertainty in human subjects research with participants of all ages, these methods can be pivotal in understanding the true level of information contained in participants' responses, despite their deviation from participants' true level of endorsement of a response. Closing out this special issue is *Latent Transition Analysis: A Statistical Method for Identifying Underlying*

Subgroups Over Time, which describes another longitudinal analytic technique aimed to assess whether and the extent to which participants shift from one category or profile to another at each subsequent measurement/observation point.

Together, this collection of methodological examinations illustrates not only the breadth of design and analysis techniques available to developmental researchers, but also the manner in which these methods may augment your existing analytic decisions. Despite the difficulty of designing and conducting an effective, efficient, and informative study in any context (much less the early childhood development context), I found this collection of manuscripts to be eminently helpful in showcasing these methodologies in theory and in practice.

SPECIAL FOCUS

Methodological Innovations for Advancing Early Childhood Educational and Psychological Research

Early Education Indirect Service Research with Generalization Data: A Systematic Review of Single-Case Design Methodological Rigor

Zachary C. LaBrot, Brittany Garza, Tyler Smith, Emily Maxime, and Abigail Lawson

Early childhood education plays a critical role in promoting young children's social-emotional, behavioral, and learning outcomes (Love, 2010; Weiland et al., 2013). To promote these vital outcomes, early childhood educators are tasked with a variety of duties, such as planning and implementing curricula, organizing various learning activities, developing routines, monitoring for early social-emotional and developmental concerns, and regularly updating and maintaining child records (U.S. Bureau of Labor Statistics, 2023). Unfortunately, high workload demand, lack of adequate preservice preparation, children's display of challenging behavior, and limited collegiality often interfere with early childhood educators' ability to adequately perform their job duties (Reinke et al., 2011; Schaak et al., 2020; Snell et al., 2012). This, in turn, often results in burnout and attrition from the field (Schaak et al., 2020).

Among the factors that lead to early childhood educators' burnout and attrition, difficulty managing children's early display of social-emotional and behavioral difficulties is often reported as the most challenging (Güder et al., 2018; Snell et al., 2012). Although early detection, prevention, and intervention efforts are impactful for improving young children's behavior, early childhood educators are typically the primary agents implementing these procedures (Reinke et al., 2011), thus adding additional work to their already demanding load. Clearly then, early childhood educators are in need of support to prevent burnout and attrition, and allow them to adequately serve their vital role of promoting young children's healthy development through the consistent implementation of evidence-based practices (EBPs; Long et al., 2016). Thus, this study aims to review and evaluate literature examining educator consultation and coaching meant to improve the implementation of EBPs within early childhood settings.

Indirect Service Delivery for Early Childhood Educators

Although pre- and in-service professional development are commonly utilized to support educators in the delivery of EBPs, they are often inadequate for changing educator practices (Flower et al., 2017; Freeman et al., 2014). This is unsurprising, as professional development activities do not allow opportunities for follow-up or support for use of EBPs in day-to-day practice (Scheeler et al., 2009). Alternatively, ongoing consultation and coaching are effective and preferred approaches for supporting educators' implementation of EBPs and improving child outcomes (Smith et al., 2021; Stormont et al., 2015).

School-based consultation involves a consultant (e.g., school psychologist) with expertise in behavior, development, and educational processes providing consultees (i.e., educators) with EBP recommendations and strategies that, in turn, are meant to address child needs. Similarly, coaching focuses on providing educators with ongoing implementation support in the delivery of EBPs. While there are slight differences between school-based consultation and coaching (see Erchul, 2023 for a thorough discussion), both share a great deal of overlap such as data-based decision making, focus on systems-level change, and prevention focus. Most importantly, school-based consultation and coaching are also considered indirect forms of service delivery in that children's needs are met by training educators to consistently deliver EBPs in day-to-day interactions as opposed to the consultant providing direct services. Furthermore, both have been found to be effective for promoting early childhood educators' use of EBPs and young children's outcomes (Smith et al., 2021; Stormont et al., 2015).

Unlike brief professional development trainings, indirect service delivery typically involves a series of problem-solving meetings aimed at addressing educators' needs (Erchul, 2023). When educators do not implement EBPs with sufficient fidelity, various implementation supports (e.g., prompts, performance feedback, behavioral skills training) are often delivered in the context of indirect service delivery. Research consistently demonstrates that indirect service delivery addresses the shortcomings of traditional professional development and is a critical mechanism for promoting educators' EBP implementation (Smith et al., 2021; Stormont et al., 2015). However, less is known about the extent to which indirect service delivery promotes educators' generalization of skills across contexts, students, and/or practices, as generalization has traditionally been overlooked in the indirect service delivery literature (Markelz et al., 2017; Robinson & Swanton, 1980; Scheeler et al., 2009).

Generalization of Educators' EBPs

Generalization is the extent to which a trained behavior occurs under different conditions from those in which the behavior was trained. For decades, the success of various behavioral interventions has been based on whether a learner generalizes behavior across time, settings, other behaviors, or people (Cooper et al., 2020; Stokes & Baer, 1977). Likewise, the success of school-based indirect service delivery can also be determined by whether educators generalize EBPs over the course of a school year (i.e., time), across different activities (i.e., settings), across other EBPs (i.e., behaviors), and with children who were not initially targeted through consultation/coaching (i.e., people).

Demonstration of educators' generalized use of EBP is critical for establishing the long-term effectiveness (i.e., EBP implementation is sustained) and efficiency (i.e., EBP spontaneously generalizes across novel contexts) of indirect service delivery modalities. Furthermore, demonstration of generalization can be considered an issue of equity. That is, educators' generalized use of EBPs allows for current and future children to be recipients of effective practices that they may have otherwise not received. Because of the importance of the collection of generalization data in indirect service delivery studies, recent research has begun to examine the extent to which these data are collected and whether indirect service delivery is effective for promoting educators' generalized outcomes.

LaBrot et al. (in press) conducted a comprehensive meta-analysis of indirect service delivery SCD studies that were published and unpublished between 1980 and 2020. Results suggested that indirect service delivery (i.e., consultation and coaching) was effective for promoting educators' generalized use of EBPs. In a subset of the data collected by LaBrot et al. (in press), Smith et al. (2023) also found that indirect service delivery was particularly effective for promoting early childhood educators' use of EBPs. Collectively, these studies demonstrate that indirect service delivery can effectively promote educators' generalized use of EBPs. However, analyses conducted in both studies excluded research that did not meet rigorous research design standards as established by the What Works Clearinghouse (WWC, 2020). Although this allowed for the unbiased analyses of research that demonstrated strong experimental control, it also served as a limitation. That is, the full extent to which the number of consultation and coaching studies collect generalization data is not fully understood, as several studies were removed from analyses due to not meeting WWC (2020) SCD standards. Furthermore, the extent to which design standards were commonly absent across studies is unknown.

Rigor of Early Childhood Education Indirect Service Delivery Research

Identifying empirically supported practices allows the mental and behavioral health field to be accountable for the various practices adopted and utilized. The emphasis on research-validated practices serves to increase the extent to which mental and behavioral health practitioners implement sound and effective practices. Even federal legislation, such as The Every Student Succeeds Act (2015), calls for the implementation of evidence-based practices in schools to improve student outcomes. The adoption and implementation of effective practices, however, requires that scientifically valid practices are available. For this reason, research design standards for evaluating various mental and behavioral health practices (e.g., assessment, intervention) have come under scrutiny to delineate practices that have legitimate scientific support. In particular, SCD research is well suited to determine the effectiveness of various indirect service delivery practices. The purpose of single-case design is to observe patterns of behavior within an individual unit (e.g., educator, child, classroom) in the presence of controlled environmental stimuli (Ledford & Gast, 2018). For this reason, SCD research has been adopted for examining a range of indirect service delivery approaches (LaBrot et al., in press).

Given its extensive application in research, The WWC developed a set of research design standards to determine the rigor of experimental research designs, including SCDs (e.g., randomized control trials, quasi-experimental designs). These standards promote the use of rigorous research designs that can establish true experimental control so that results can be generalized to the larger population (WWC, 2022). However, SCDs have been criticized for including fewer participants than randomized control trials and quasi-experimental designs, and thus less generalizability. As such, the use of WWC standards to guide the development of rigorous SCDs that establish true experimental control is vital to support their use in evaluating various behavioral phenomena. Since the development of these standards, systematic reviews of various practices, such as self-management (Maggin et al., 2013), social stories (Wahman et al., 2022), and social skills training interventions (Dong et al., 2023), among others, have been conducted to determine whether studies evaluating these practices meet WWC SCD standards.

This has also occurred within the indirect service delivery literature bases (e.g., Fallon et al., 2015, 2018). However, to our knowledge, the WWC research design standards have not been applied to indirect service delivery research with specific focus on early childhood educators' generalized outcomes. This is problematic, as it does little to guide future research in the way of informing research design standards that should be included in replication studies and novel iterations of indirect service delivery research. Given the importance of the collection of generalization data in indirect service delivery in early childhood education research, additional rigorously conducted experimental research is needed. However, to accomplish this, the current status of the methodological rigor of indirect service delivery research in early childhood education must be first summarized and disseminated.

Purpose

The purpose of this systematic review was to identify early childhood educator indirect service delivery research, with a focus on studies that collected data on educators' generalized outcomes. Of specific interest were research design characteristics and whether these research designs met quality rigor standards as outlined by the WWC (e.g., Dong et al., 2023). The fundamental goals of this manuscript are twofold: (1) first, we aim to make a call to action for indirect service delivery researchers to collect data on educators' generalized outcomes; (2) second, we use the results of the following review to provide specific guidance to future researchers on strategies to conduct more rigorous indirect service delivery research that examines educators' generalized outcomes. The following research questions were addressed:
1. To what extent does the evidence base for indirect service delivery meet WWC design standards that evaluated early childhood educators' generalized outcomes?
2. What are the methodological strengths and areas of improvement for the included studies?

Method

The present study was part of a larger meta-analysis focused on the effects of school-based indirect service delivery for promoting educators' use of EBPs (LaBrot et al., in press; Smith et al., 2023). For purposes of the current study, all studies focused on *early childhood educators* and were identified and analyzed to answer our research questions. In the following sections, we first describe methods and procedures from our larger meta-analysis, followed by selection and analyses. Compilation of the current meta-analytic database included three steps: (1) literature search, (2) identification of studies, and (3) study coding. Between three and four individuals (i.e., study authors and trained graduate students) were involved at each stage of the process.

Literature Search Procedures

Three central search procedures were used comprehensively search the relevant literature: electronic database searching, hand searching of journals, and reference list searching of previous reviews. First, five electronic databases (i.e., *Academic Search Premiere, ERIC, APA PsychInfo, and APA PsychArticles*) were searched using multiple search term parameters and combinations. Specific search terms included a combination of search strings (e.g., "teacher*," "educator*," "school* staff," "school*, "consult*," "coach*," "behavior* manage*," strategy," "class* discipline," "generalization," "generalize," "maintenance," "maintain," and "fidelity"). Search parameters were also limited to studies written in English and those conducted from 1980 to 2020. The year 1980 was chosen as a starting point to build off Robinson and Swanton's 1980 work (LaBrot et al., in press; Smith et al., 2023). To gather grey literature, we also conducted searches through the online database *ProQuest: Dissertation & Theses* and Google Scholar. Second, we conducted hand searches of 15 relevant journals focused on mental and behavioral health services in schools (e.g., *Journal of Behavioral Education, School Psychology Review, School Psychology*), teacher education and training (e.g., *Journal of Teacher Education, Teaching and Teacher Education*), and behavioral psychology (e.g., *Behavioral Interventions, Journal of Applied Behavior Analysis*). Third, we searched reference lists of previously published relevant meta-analyses and reviews (e.g., Collier-Meek et al., 2018; Reddy et al., 2000).

Study Identification

Search procedures yielded 1,577 journal articles, book chapters, and dissertations/theses for review (1,226 identified through electronic database searching and 351 records identified through other sources). See Figure 1 for an overview of search and screening processes at each stage of the study. Records located through search procedures were then retained and reviewed for potential inclusion following a two-step approach with increasing specificity – abstract screening and full-text reviews. Details of screening and reviewing performed at each step are described below.

Figure 1
Flowchart of Search and Screening

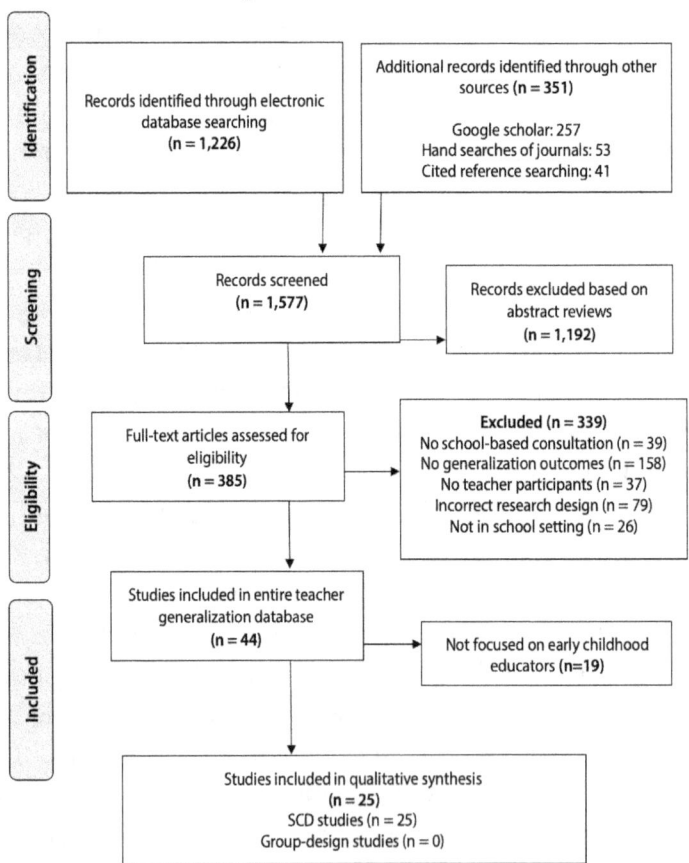

Abstract screening. Abstracts were independently screened by study authors based on two broad inclusion criteria: (1) the study must have assessed educator outcomes and (2) the study must have involved school-based indirect service delivery. Approximately 30% of all abstracts were double-screened and compared for inconsistencies during weekly research team meetings. When disagreements occurred, the research team discussed the disagreements until consensus was reached. Inclusion/exclusion agreement was 94% for abstracts that were double screened. 385 articles were retained at this stage based on the two criteria described above.

Full-text reviews. The second step of the identification process involved two research team members independently reviewing each full-text article identified as potentially relevant during the abstract screening stage. Specifically, research team members were trained to ensure studies met the following criteria:

(1) The study must have included consultation/coaching or training/professional development of school personnel aimed at indirectly supporting children's behavioral or social-emotional development (e.g., behavioral consultation with a school psychologist to address child disruptive behavior, educator training in classroom management practices);

(2) Recipients of consultation/coaching or training/professional development must have been school-based personnel (including teachers, pre-service teachers, teacher aides, pre-service or in-service clinicians [e.g., behavior analysts], paraprofessionals, speech pathologists, before- and after-school staff, classroom volunteers, or other school staff);

(3) The study must have occurred in a school setting (e.g., classroom, playground, gym; Cole et al., 2000) focused on early childhood care and education (any program below kindergarten level);

(4) The study needed to include at least one outcome measurement assessing the generalization of school personnel practices (i.e., the ability to use and transfer practices across multiple

participants [e.g., children], settings [e.g., different activities], and/or behaviors [e.g., praise, effective instruction];

(5) The study must have included either a single-case experimental design (SCD) or group-design (i.e., experimental or quasi-experimental design) that compared groups receiving consultation/coaching or training/professional development with one or more control groups. No group designs met inclusion criteria. 48 SCD studies met our inclusion criteria. Of the 48 SCD studies reviewed, 25 studies met inclusion criteria.

Study Coding

Variable coding. All studies were coded to extract information regarding pertinent study characteristics. Study authors created and developed a codebook that included multiple sections designed to focus on study-, participant-, and outcome-level variables. The codebook was developed by creating initial codes, testing said codes, and revising codes as necessary (codebook available from first author upon request). Once the codebook was developed, coders independently reviewed studies and met weekly to discuss disagreements and reach a consensus. See Table 1 for the coding scheme used for this review. In particular, articles were coded based on consultee type (e.g., teacher, teacher aide, preservice teacher), indirect service delivery characteristics (e.g., in situ training, behavioral skills training), indirect service delivery type (i.e., consultation or coaching), and the form of generalization outcome measured (e.g., across settings, across children). Additionally, articles were coded for consultee characteristics, such as race/ethnicity and gender. All studies were double-coded and percent agreement was 97%, indicating high agreement among reviewers.

Table 1
Coding scheme for the present study

Generalization characteristics	
Outcome subtypes	• *Behavior specific praise* (i.e., providing students with praise statements that explicitly describe the behavior being praised [e.g., "Thank you for walking over here so quietly."]; Allday et al., 2012) • *Behavior analytic procedures* (i.e., assessment or intervention procedure implemented by a registered behavior technician or board-certified behavior analyst) • *Individual support plan* (i.e., multi-component behavior intervention plan developed for an individual student) • Instructional practices (i.e., teacher tasks, methods, and activities that guide and support student learning within classroom instruction [e.g., problem-solving, problem-posing, instruction giving, model-eliciting activities, information sharing]; Bicer, 2021)
Form	• *Across students* • *Across activities/periods* • *Across non-classroom setting*

Table 1 continued

Consultee characteristics	
Gender	• *Female* • *Male*
Consultee type	• *Preservice* • *Teacher* • *Teacher aid* • *Paraeducator*
Race and ethnicity	• *American Indian/Alaska Native* • *Asian/Asian Pacific* • *Black/African American* • *Latinx* • *White* • *Multi-racial*
Classroom type	• *General education* • *Special education* • *Inclusive education* • *Head Start/Early Head Start*

Study characteristics	
Publication status	• *Journal Article* • *Thesis/Dissertation*

Consultation and coaching practices	
Component	• *In situ training* (i.e., the teaching of a skill in the context with which it is intended to be used [e.g., prompting teachers to praise students via a bug-in-the-ear device during ongoing classroom activities]; LaBrot et al., 2016)

Consultation and coaching practices	
	- *Performance feedback* (i.e., a critique of observed behavior that is immediate, specific, positive, and corrective as needed, designed to move the recipient toward a desired behavior or performance; Cornelius & Nagro, 2014)
- *Behavioral skills training* (i.e., combination of instructions, modeling, rehearsal, and performance feedback; Kirkpatrick et al., 2019)
- *Self-evaluation* (i.e., reflecting on one's own behavior, recording those observations, and reviewing and analyzing those data to make decisions regarding how to improve one's behavior; Lynes et al., 2012)
- *Video modeling* (i.e., viewing someone else or one's self demonstrating correct implementation of a desired behavior or performance; Brock et al., 2018)
- *Didactic training* (i.e., a method in which concepts, practices, and techniques are explained to clients, and instructions are provided in verbal and/or written form; American Psychological Association, n.d.)
Generalization programming efforts included	Did the study incorporate intentional efforts to promote or support teacher use of generalized practices beyond the original context in which practices were trained? - *Yes* - *No*

Application of What Works Clearinghouse standards. Primary analysis of the WWC standards were based on the What Works Clearinghouse Procedures and Standards Handbook, Version 5.0 (WWC, 2022), while secondary analysis was based on Version 4.1 (WWC, 2020). Each study was coded for degree of meeting each set of overall standards (i.e., without reservations, with reservations, and does not meet). When multiple dependent variables were included in a study, the designated primary dependent variable was evaluated. If a primary dependent variable was not explicitly stated, a primary variable was surmised based on the primary research question. If a study included two experiments, each experiment was evaluated separately (as in the case of Peck et al., 1989). This resulted in a total of 26 evaluations across 25 articles. Slight differences exist between the 2022 and 2020 WWC criteria and their evaluation of inter-observer agreement, adequate data collection, and risk of bias. For that reason, both criteria were evaluated to discern patterns of rigor and/or shortcomings. Both 2022 and 2020 were coded, as the 2022 criteria are so new that it was unlikely included studies would meet 2022 standards given the search span from 1980-2020.

The protocol developed for the analysis of the 2022 design standards was designed to adhere to six key methodological criteria as described by the WWC Handbook Version 5.0. The first four were scored using a dichotomous scale (i.e., present, not present) and included the following: (1) inter-observer agreement was collected in each phase and in 20% of data points across overall outcome variables and meets 80% agreement if measured by percent agreement or .60 if measured by Cohen's kappa; (2) researchers provided data in a graphical and/or tabular format; (3) the independent variable was systematically manipulated, with researchers determining when independent variable conditions change; and (4) there were limited residual treatment effects for designs with two or more intervention conditions (Maggin et al., 2013). If any study was determined to not meet any of these criteria, it was classified as not meeting design standards. The fifth criterion related to the total number of data points per phase and was scored as a trichotomous variable (i.e., Meets Standards without Reservations, Meets Standards with Reservations, and Does Not Meet Standards; Maggin et al., 2013) for multiple baseline and probe designs, as these were the only designs identified in the search. Within this criterion, the design had to have allowed at least three attempts to demonstrate the intervention effect at three different points of time. If this criterion was not met, the design was considered to have not met standards. Designs were classified as Meets Standards without Reservations if the first baseline phase within each tier had at least six data points and all subsequent phases had at least five data points. Additionally, any phases with three or more data points with zero within-phase variability also counted towards Meeting Standards. For multiple probe designs specifically, to be classified as Meets without Reservations, each tier must have had three data points in the first three sessions with three consecutive data points prior to introducing the independent variable. Failure to meet both of these requirements in addition to the multiple baseline requirements would result in classification as Does Not Meet Standards. Designs were classified as Meets Standards with Reservations if there were at least three or more data points per phase. Finally, designs that included fewer than three data points per phase were classified as Does Not Meet Standards (Maggin et al., 2013). If a study met the above standards without reservations, a sixth criterion evaluating the limited risk of bias was considered. This evaluation involved determining the non-presence of undesirable baseline trend and non-overlap of outcome variables across baseline and intervention phases. The second author coded this variable according to visual analysis of non-overlap due to an inability to calculate non-overlap without access to each study's raw data.

    Coding schemes were adapted from those of Dong et al. (2023). The codebook evaluated six design standards (DS) as outlined in the WWC 2022 standards: a sufficient amount of inter-observer agreement (IOA) and high agreement (DS-1), results displayed visually

(DS-2), researcher manipulated the independent variable (DS-3), no residual treatment effects for studies with two or more intervention conditions (DS-4), more than three attempts to demonstrate effects across at least three timepoints and adequate data collected per phase (DS-5), and evidence of limited risk of bias (DS-6; Dong et al., 2023).

Analysis of the WWC (2020) standards was almost the same, apart from including a minimum of six data points in baseline phases, the zero within-phase variability consideration, and slight changes in IOA standards. Specifically, the 2020 standards only call for a minimum of five baseline data points and do not have the zero within-phase variability consideration. The WWC (2020) standards described IOA as 20% collected for baseline and intervention phases separately and minimal standards met for all phases and cases as well as each DV. Further, there is no risk of bias consideration in the 2020 standards.

Coder agreement. Design standard coding was conducted by the first and second authors. Both authors designed the coding protocol and conducted practice coding until reliability was obtained. Coding practice included coding a practice article independently and then both coders reviewing codes. Disagreements were discussed and a consensus was reached. The second author coded all articles for the WWC design standards. The first author coded 28% ($n = 7$) of articles for both 2022 and 2020 WWC standards. Percentage agreement was 96% and 95% for 2022 and 2020 standards, respectively, indicating a high level of reliability. The first author was a doctoral level, licensed psychologist and assistant professor with over 10 years of experience conducting and reviewing single-case design research. The second author was a Ph.D. student in school psychology, board certified behavior analyst, and had over 12 years of experience providing direct and/or consultative early childhood behavioral support.

Results
Study Characteristics

Overall, all studies either utilized a multiple baseline (72%, $n = 18$) or multiple probe (28%, $n = 7$) design. Of the types of indirect service delivery, 13 (52%) utilized a form of consultation while 12 (48%) utilized some form of coaching. Across most studies, in-service teachers served as the consultees, with four (16%) including pre-service teachers (Barton et al., 2018; Coogle et al., 2015, 2020; Rakap, 2017), one including teacher aides (4%; Frantz, 2017), one including paraeducators (4%; Hall et al., 2010), and two including a combination of various consultees (8%; LaBrot et al., 2020; Lerman et al., 2004). Most generalization outcomes measured included various instructional practices (56%, $n = 14$). Implementation supports utilized within consultation or coaching included in situ training (36%, $n = 9$), performance feedback (20%, $n = 5$), video modeling (4%, $n = 1$), behavioral skills training (52%, $n = 13$), self-evaluation (4%, $n = 1$), training protocol (4%, $n = 1$), and didactic training (4%, $n = 1$). See Table 2 for study characteristics data.

Summary of 2022 and 2020 WWC Standards

For the 2022 WWC criteria, 7.69% of the studies ($n = 2$) were classified as having Met Standards without Reservations, 46.15% ($n = 12$) Met Standards with Reservations, and 46.15% ($n = 12$) Did Not Meet Design Standards. For the 2020 WWC criteria, 19.32% of the studies ($n = 5$) were classified as having Met Standards without Reservations, 34.62% ($n = 9$) Met Standards with Reservations, and 46.15% ($n = 12$) Did Not Meet Standards.

Table 2
Characteristics of Included Studies

Author(s)	Study type	Design	Class-room type	Number of consultees	Indirect service type	Consultee type	Consultee race/eth.	Consultee gender (% female)	Gen. outcome(s)	Gen. type	Implementation support
Barton et al. (2016)	Journal article	Multiple baseline	Inclusive	3	Coach.	Preservice	NR	100%	IP	Act.; Chi.	In situ; PF
Bose-Deakins (2006)	Thesis/Dissertation	Multiple probe	Head Start	3	Cons.	Teacher	100% Bl.	100%	IP	Act.	VM
Coogle et al. (2015)	Journal article	Multiple probe	Inclusive	3	Coach.	Preservice	100% Wh.	100%	IP	Act.	In situ
Coogle et al. (2020)	Journal article	Multiple probe	Inclusive	3	Coach.	Preservice	100% Wh.	100%	IP	Act.	PF
Crawford (2018)	Thesis/Dissertation	Multiple probe	Head Start	3	Coach.	Teacher	75% Bl.; 25% Other	100%	IP	Chi./Beh.	BST
Duncan et al. (2013)	Journal article	Multiple baseline	Head Start	3	Cons.	Teacher	100% Wh.	100%	BSP	Stud.	BST
Frantz (2017)	Thesis/Dissertation	Multiple baseline	Inclusive	4	Coach.	Teacher aid	75% Wh.; 25% As.	100%	BAP	Stud.	BST; In situ
Freeland (2003)	Thesis/Dissertation	Multiple baseline	Head Start	3	Cons.	Teacher	100% Bl.	100%	BSP; GP; IP	Act.	In situ
Fullerton et al. (2009)	Journal article	Multiple baseline	General	4	Cons.	Teacher	50% Wh.; 50% Bl	75%	GP; BSP	Act.	BST
Gouvousis (2012)	Thesis/Dissertation	Multiple baseline	Special	1	Cons.	Teacher	NR	NR	BAP; BSP; IP	Act.	BST

Author(s)	Study type	Design	Class-room type	Number of consultees	Indirect service type	Consultee type	Consultee race/eth.	Consultee gender (% female)	Gen. outcome(s)	Gen. type	Implementation support
Hall et al. (2010)	Journal article	Multiple baseline	Special/Home-based	6	Coach.	Para	NR	83%	IP	Act.	BST
Hemmeter et al. (2015)	Journal article	Multiple probe	Inclusive	3	Coach.	Teacher	100% Wh.	100%	IP	Act.	In situ
Hundert (2007)	Journal article	Multiple baseline	Inclusive	4	Cons.	Teacher	NR	100%	IP	Act.	BST
Kaiser et al. (1993)	Journal article	Multiple baseline	Special	3	Cons.	Teacher	NR	100%	IP	Act.	BST
LaBrot et al. (2021)	Journal article	Multiple baseline	Head Start	4	Cons.	Combination	100% Bl.	100%	BSP	Act.	In situ
Lerman et al. (2004)	Journal article	Multiple baseline	Special	4	Coach.	Combination	NR	NR	IP	Chi./Act.	BST
Lynes (2012)	Thesis/Dissertation	Multiple baseline	Head Start	6	Coach.	Teacher	NR	NR	IP	Act.	BST; SE
Madigan (2012)	Thesis/Dissertation	Multiple baseline	Special	5	Coach.	Teacher	NR	NR	BSP; IP	Act.	BST
Marsicano et al. (2015)	Journal article	Multiple baseline	Head Start	3	Cons.	Teacher	66% Wh.; 33% Bl.	66%	IP	Act.	BST; PF

Table 2 continued

Author(s)	Study type	Design	Class-room type	Number of consultees	Indirect service type	Consultee type	Consultee race/eth.	Consultee gender (% female)	Gen. outcome(s)	Gen. type	Implementation support
Peck et al. (1989)	Journal article	Multiple baseline	General	3	Cons.	Teacher	NR	100%	IP	Act.	DT; TP
Pellecchia et al. (2011)	Journal article	Multiple baseline	Special	4	Cons.	Teacher	33% Wh.; 42% Bl.; 17% Lx; 8% As.	100%	IP	Chi.	DT; PF
Rakap (2017)	Journal article	Multiple baseline	Inclusive	3	Coach.	Preservice	NR	100%	BAP	Act.	In situ
Shepley (2019)	Thesis/Dissertation	Multiple probe	General	4	Coach.	Teacher	100% Wh.	75%	BAP	Chi.	BST
Watkins-Emonet (2001)	Thesis/Dissertation	Multiple baseline	Head Start	2	Cons.	Teacher	100%Bl.	100%	GP; BSP	Act.	In situ
Wimberly (2016)	Thesis/Dissertation	Multiple baseline	Head Start	4	Cons.	Teacher	100%Bl.	100%	IP	Act.	In situ; PF

Note: coach. = coaching; cons. = consultation; NR = not reported; PF = performance feedback; VM = video modeling; BST = behavioral skills training; DT = didactic training; TP = training protocol; In situ = in situ training; SE = Self- evaluation; Act. = activity/setting; Chi. = children; Beh. = behavior; GP = general praise; BSP = behavior specific praise; IP = instructional practices; BAP = behavior analytic procedures; Lx = Latinx; Bl. = Black; As. = Asian; Wh. = white; Multi. = multiracial; Para. = paraeducator

What Works Clearinghouse 2022 Standards

See Table 3 for 2022 WWC standards coding results. Of the dichotomous variables, failing to systematically manipulate the independent variable was found to be the primary reason for not meeting 2022 design standards (23.08%, $n = 6$). Most of the studies that fall into this category did not identify phase change decisions based on visual analysis, and/or implemented didactic training to all participants without regard to participant-level baseline patterns of responding. The results for each of six design standards are outlined below.

Inter-observer agreement (DS-1). Most studies (88.46%, $n = 23$) reported IOA on 20% or more of their data and met 80% agreement or .60 for Cohen's Kappa. The 2022 IOA criterion calls for meeting minimum standards for each outcome variable. Each of the studies that did not meet this criterion did not report IOA for each dependent variable and the overall ranges fell below 80% (Hall et al., 2010; Hundert, 2007; Peck et al. [study 2], 1989).

Results visually displayed (DS-2). All studies (100%, $n = 26$) displayed results in a table and/or graph.

Systematic manipulation of the independent variable (DS-3). Several studies did not systematically introduce the independent variable for each participant (23.08%, $n = 6$). Three studies introduced the independent variable after a set number of data points as opposed to using visual analysis to make phase change decisions (Crawford, 2018; Kaiser et al., 1993; Lerman et al., 2004). Hundert (2007) collected an adequate amount of data but did not describe a systematic manipulation of the independent variable and determinants for phase change decisions. Freeland (2002) did not describe phase change decisions and intervention was not introduced in a staggered fashion. Lastly, Hall et al. (2010) implemented didactic training at the same time point for all participants, and the independent variable was not introduced in a staggered fashion.

No residual treatment effects (DS-4). No studies were eligible for this criterion due to being either a multiple baseline or multiple probe design and not comparing two or more intervention conditions, rendering this criterion irrelevant.

Adequate data collection (DS-5). Several studies did not meet this criterion Without Reservations (38.46%, $n = 10$). Of these studies, four did not Meet Standards due to having less than three attempts to replicate treatment effects across three time periods (Fullerton et al., 2010; Freeland 2002; Peck et al. [study 2], 1989; Watkins-Emonet 2000). For example, Freeland (2002) described time limits and schedule changes in the school year that restricted data collection, thus rendering the data inadequate for a complete multiple baseline design. Six studies simply did not collect enough data points across baseline and/or intervention phases (Crawford, 2018; Hall et al., 2010; Lerman et al., 2004; Lynes, 2012; Madigan, 2012; Marsicano et al., 2015).

Several studies Met Standards with Reservations (38.46%, $n = 10$). These studies collected between three and five data points per baseline and intervention phases (Barton et al., 2018; Bose-Deakins, 2005; Coogle et al., 2015; Coogle et al., 2020; Duncan et al., 2013; Hemmeter et al., 2015; Frantz, 2017; Rakap, 2017; Wimberley, 2016). One study Met this Standard with Reservations due to inadequate data collection in the intervention phase (Frantz, 2017). Additionally, two of these studies utilized a multiple probe design in which the WWC standards call for at least three consecutive probes collected in the first three sessions across all cases, and sufficient data were not collected according to this criterion (Bose-Deakins, 2005; Hemmeter et al., 2015). Multiple probe design standards also call for at least three overlapping probes across phases in baseline and three probes collected consecutively in the first three sessions, and the study by Shepley (2019) did not meet this criterion. Six studies (23.08%) Met Standards without Reservations for adequate data collection (Pellechia et al., 2011; Peck et al. [study 1], 1989; Kaiser et al., 1993; Hundert, 2007; Gouvousis, 2011; LaBrot et al., 2020). Of these, LaBrot et al. (2020) did not collect six data points in baseline, however, the five data points that were collected demonstrated zero variability.

Limited risk of bias (DS-6). Of the studies evaluated, any that Met Standards without Reservations for the other standards were eligible to be coded for limited risk of bias. Five studies were evaluated for this design standard, and three met this standard. This qualified these three studies as meeting 2022 WWC Standards without Reservations (Barton et al., 2018; LaBrot et al., 2020; Peck et al. [study 1], 1989).

Table 3
What Works Clearinghouse 5.0 (2022) Standards

Study	Design	OV	DS-1	DS-2	DS-3	DS-4*	DS-5	DS-6**
Barton et al. (2016)	MBD	1	2	2	2	n	1	n
Bose-Deakins (2006)	MPD	1	2	2	2	n	1	n
Coogle et al. (2015)	MPD	1	2	2	2	n	1	n
Coogle et al. (2020)	MPD	1	2	2	2	n	1	n
Crawford (2018)	MPD	0	2	2	0	n	0	n
Duncan et al. (2013)	MBD	1	2	2	2	n	1	n
Frantz (2017)	MBD	1	2	2	2	n	1	n
Freeland (2003)	MBD	0	2	2	0	n	0	n
Fullerton et al. (2009)	MBD	0	2	2	2	n	0	n
Gouvousis (2012)	MBD	1	2	2	2	n	2	0

Table 3 continued

Study	Design	OV	DS-1	DS-2	DS-3	DS-4*	DS-5	DS-6**
Hall et al. (2010)	MBD	0	0	2	0	n	0	n
Hemmeter et al. (2015)	MPD	1	2	2	2	n	1	n
Hundert (2007)	MBD	0	0	2	0	n	2	n
Kaiser et al. (1993)	MBD	0	2	2	0	n	2	n
LaBrot et al. (2020)	MBD	2	2	2	2	n	2	2
Lerman et al. (2004)	MBD	0	2	2	0	n	0	n
Lynes (2012)	MBD	0	2	2	2	n	0	n
Madigan (2012)	MPD	0	2	2	2	n	0	n
Marsicano et al. (2015)	MBD	0	2	2	2	n	0	n
Peck et al. (1989) - 1	MBD	2	2	2	2	n	2	2
Peck et al. (1989) - 2	MBD	0	0	2	2	n	0	n
Pellechia et al. (2011)	MBD	1	2	2	2	n	2	0
Rakap (2017)	MBD	1	2	2	2	n	1	n
Shepley (2019)	MPD	1	2	2	2	n	1	n

Study	Design	OV	DS-1	DS-2	DS-3	DS-4*	DS-5	DS-6**
Watkins-Emonet (2001)	MBD	0	2	2	2	n	0	n
Wimberly (2016)	MBD	1	2	2	2	n	1	n

Note: OV= overall; DS-1= IOA; DS-2= visual display; DS-3= systematically manipulated IV;
DS-4= no residual treatment; DS-5= adequate data collection; DS-6= limited risk of bias;
2= meets without reservations; 1= meets with reservations; 0= does not meet; n= not applicable;
MBD= multiple baseline design; MPD= multiple probe design;
*Does not apply to MBD or MPD;
**Only coded if meets standards without reservations through DS-5

What Works Clearinghouse 2020 Standards

See Table 4 for 2020 WWC standards coding results. Many design standards outlined in the 2020 What Works Clearinghouse design standards overlap with the 2022 design standards. These standards include that the results were visually displayed (DS-1), the independent variable was systematically manipulated (DS-2), and that there were no residual treatment effects (DS-4) For that reason, no further discussion regarding these design standards is included.

Overall, five studies Met Standards without Reservations (Coogle et al., 2015; Gouvousis, 2011; LaBrot et al., 2020; Pellachia et al., 2011; Wimberly, 2016). In congruence with 2022 WWC evaluation results, systematically introducing the independent variable was found to be the primary reason for not meeting 2020 design standards (26.92%, $n = 7$).

Inter-observer agreement (DS-3). Most studies (88.46%, $n = 23$) reported IOA on 20% or more of their data and met 80% agreement or .60 for Cohen's Kappa. Of the studies that did not meet this criterion, the main findings were that IOA had not been collected for 20% of baseline and intervention phases (Hall et al., 2010). At times it was unclear whether at least 20% IOA had been collected and/or a minimum of 80% agreement had not been reached (Hundert, 2007; Peck et al., 1989).

Adequate data collection (DS-5). Several of the studies evaluated did not meet this criterion without reservations (31%, $n = 8$). Of these studies, five did not meet this criterion due to having less than three data points per phase (Crawford, 2018; Lerman et al., 2004; Lynes, 2012; Madigan, 2012; Marsicano et al., 2015). Three did not demonstrate at least three replications of treatment effects across at least three points in time (Freeland, 2002; Fullerton et al., 2009; Watkins-Emonet, 2000).

Several studies Met this Standard with Reservations (35%, $n = 9$). One study no longer Met this Standard without Reservations due to WWC 2020 standards not providing an exception for adequate data collection being met due to zero variability, but did meet this criterion with reservations (Peck at al. [study 1], 1989). Like the 2022 WWC criteria, the 2020 multiple probe design standards call for at least three overlapping probes across phases in baseline and three probes collected consecutively in the first three sessions. Three studies Met this Standard with Reservations (Bose-Deakins, 2005; Hemmeter et al., 2015; Shepley, 2019). Lastly, numerous studies simply did not collect enough data per phase (Barton et al., 2018; Coogle et al., 2020; Duncan et al., 2013; Frantz, 2017; Hall et al., 2010). Nine studies (35%) Met this Standard without Reservations.

Table 4
What Works Clearinghouse 4.1 (2020) Standards

Study	Design	OV	DS-1	DS-2	DS-3	DS-4*	DS-5
Barton et al. (2016)	MBD	1	2	2	2	n	1
Bose-Deakins (2006)	MPD	1	2	2	2	n	1
Coogle et al. (2015)	MPD	2	2	2	2	n	2

Single-Case Design Methodological Rigor 27

Study	Design	OV	DS-1	DS-2	DS-3	DS-4*	DS-5
Coogle et al. (2020)	MPD	1	2	2	2	n	1
Crawford (2018)	MPD	0	2	0	2	n	0
Duncan et al. (2013)	MBD	1	2	2	2	n	1
Frantz (2017)	MBD	1	2	2	2	n	1
Freeland (2003)	MBD	0	2	0	2	n	0
Fullerton et al. (2009)	MBD	0	2	2	2	n	0
Gouvousis (2012)	MBD	2	2	2	2	n	2
Hall et al. (2010)	MBD	0	0	2	0	n	0
Hemmeter et al. (2015)	MPD	1	2	2	2	n	1
Hundert (2007)	MBD	0	2	0	0	n	2
Kaiser et al. (1993)	MBD	0	2	0	2	n	2
LaBrot et al. (2020)	MBD	2	2	2	2	n	2
Lerman et al. (2004)	MBD	0	2	0	2	n	0
Lynes (2012)	MBD	0	2	2	2	n	0
Madigan (2012)	MPD	0	2	2	2	n	0
Marsicano et al. (2015)	MBD	0	2	2	2	n	0

Table 4 continued

Study	Design	OV	DS-1	DS-2	DS-3	DS-4*	DS-5
Peck et al. (1989) - 1	MBD	1	2	2	2	n	1
Peck et al. (1989) - 2	MBD	0	2	2	0	n	2
Pellechia et al. (2011)	MBD	2	2	2	2	n	2
Rakap (2017)	MBD	1	2	2	2	n	2
Shepley (2019)	MPD	1	2	2	2	n	1
Watkins-Emonet (2001)	MBD	0	2	2	2	n	0
Wimberly (2016)	MBD	2	2	2	2	n	2

Note: OV= overall; DS-1= visual display; DS-2= systematically manipulated; DS-3= IOA;
DS-4= no residual treatment; DS-5= adequate data collection
2= meets without reservations; 1= meets with reservations; 0= does not meet; n= not applicable;
MBD= multiple baseline design; MPA= multiple prove design
*Does not apply to MBD or MPD

Discussion

Early childhood education is important for supporting young children's vital social-emotional, behavioral, and learning outcomes, with early childhood educators playing a critical role in promoting these outcomes. Consistent, educator-implemented EBPs are a catalyst for promoting these vital outcomes. Yet, early childhood educators often lack the training and support need to consistently implement EBPs (Flower et al., 2017; Freeman et al., 2014; Scheeler et al., 2009). Fortunately, indirect service delivery practices, such as consultation and coaching, are effective methods for promoting early childhood educators' EBP implementation (Smith et al., 2021; Stormont et al., 2015) and their generalized outcomes (LaBrot et al., in press; Smith et al., 2023). However, less is known about the methodological rigor of the research on indirect service delivery by early childhood educators that collected educators' generalized outcomes. As such, the purpose of this study was to (1) identify the methodological rigor of this data base based on WWC 2022 and 2020 standards and (2) identify the various strengths and weaknesses of these research designs.

Collectively, included studies utilized either a multiple baseline or multiple probe design, which is commensurate with the indirect service delivery literature, given that the effects of training cannot be withdrawn. Furthermore, there was an even split of consultation and coaching studies. Across included studies, nearly half did not meet 2022 and 2020 WWC design standards. This is concerning, as a large portion of the early education indirect service delivery literature base that collected generalization data is not rigorous enough to confirm whether indirect service delivery truly resulted in educators' generalized outcomes. In contrast, a little more than half of the included studies met WWC criteria With Reservations and Without Reservations, providing some relatively convincing evidence of the effects of indirect service delivery on early childhood educators' generalized outcomes. The fact that nearly half of included studies did not meet design standards is unsurprising, given that the WWC only initially introduced quality research design standards for SCD research in 2010 (Kratochwill et al., 2010) and several of these studies were conducted before that time. Additionally, only eight studies even mentioned WWC standards, of which seven referenced the 2010 standards and one referenced the 2020 standards while they were still being piloted. Regardless, results of this study clearly indicate that more attention to the rigor with which early childhood education indirect service delivery studies that examine generalization outcomes is needed. Furthermore, given the relatively small amount of early education indirect service delivery research that collected data on generalization, additional research that collects data on educators' generalized outcomes is sorely needed.

Regarding individual WWC (2022) standards, all studies displayed their data visually, did not have residual treatment effects, and had limited risk of bias. This likely occurred due to the nature of the types of SCDs utilized (i.e., multiple baseline, multiple probe), which require graphical display of data and render residual treatment effects moot unless another treatment is being evaluated. Furthermore, studies that met all other design standards did not have issues with residual treatment effects likely due to the fact that rigorous research designs controlled for this. The most common design element that did not meet 2022 standards was researchers systematically manipulating the independent variable. The most common reason this occurred was due to researchers implementing intervention after a set amount of data points, regardless of visual analysis (Crawford, 2018; Kaiser et al., 1993; Lerman et al., 2004). This is problematic as it does not control for environmental events that could result in spontaneous improvement.

Concerning the 2020 standards, visual display of data, residual treatment effects, and systematic manipulation of the independent variable did not differ from the 2022 standards across all studies. IOA standards were met as often as the 2022 standards. This is interesting, as the 2022 IOA standards appear to be less stringent than the 2020 standards. Although the 2022 standards require IOA data collection in each phase, they do not specify what percentage is necessary per phase. This is a potential concern, as future studies may have less IOA data collection in certain phases, thus resulting in concerns regarding the reliability of measurement and ultimately, validity of study outcomes. Finally, more studies met the 2020 WWC standards for containing an adequate number of data points than the 2022 standards. This occurred because the 2020 WWC standards did not call for studies with three to four baseline data points per phase to be classified as Meeting Standards without Reservations based on zero variability, and at least five data points must have been collected across baseline and intervention phases.

Limitations and Future Directions

There are at least two notable limitations that warrant discussion. First, the analyses conducted in this study only included SCD research studies. Although this is unsurprising given the nature of behavioral teacher training studies, it potentially excludes other designs (e.g., randomized control trials) that examined early childhood indirect service delivery and collected generalization data. We attempted to capture all research designs examining this, but only SCDs met our study's inclusion criteria. As such, future research should seek to have broader inclusion criteria such that other designs are included. Second, the 2010 WWC design standards were not considered in this study. They were not considered because they were identical to the 2020 standards but did not include standards for data being displayed graphically and consideration of residual treatment effects. These were consistently met by the 2020 standards, and therefore an analysis of the 2010 standards was deemed unnecessary. However, because the 2010 standards were not considered, there is still a possibility of an empirical historical bias. Future research should apply all three design standards to control for potential historical bias.

Implications

The results of this study offer important implications for designing future SCD indirect service delivery in early childhood education research that seeks to collect generalization data. These implications are discussed below based on common WWC standards that included studies did not achieve. As such, commonly achieved standards such as graphically displaying data and residual treatment effects will not be discussed in depth. That said, we strongly encourage researchers to display their data both graphically and numerically (i.e., means, ranges) so indirect service delivery scholars and practitioners can interpret data comprehensively. Moreover, residual treatment effects did not apply to the studies included in this review, as no study compared more than one treatment. This is unsurprising, as alternating treatment designs are far more likely to experience the threat of residual treatment effects (Barlow & Hayes, 1979; Maggin et al., 2022; Shapiro et al., 1982). However, it is certainly possible that future indirect service delivery studies include a comparison of different implementation supports on early educators' EBP implementation; as such, SCD research comparing more than one implementation support should collect at least five data points per implementation support with no more than two consecutive conditions in a randomized fashion (Kratochwill & Levin, 2010; WWC, 2022). Below, more specific recommendations for developing rigorous research designs are discussed.

Establishing IOA. Although included studies mostly met IOA standards for both 2022 and 2020 standards, the 2022 standards could potentially lead to some phases containing less IOA data. For example, a baseline phase that only included 10% of data points with IOA data and a consultation/treatment phase of 30% would still yield a 20% criterion. However, the reliability of the data in the baseline phase would be substantially lower and thus call into question the reliability of data collection for a given outcome in that phase. Therefore, we recommend that future researchers conducting early education indirect service delivery research adhere to the 2020 WWC standards, such that IOA data are collected for a minimum of 20% of data points per phase. This would still allow for research to meet 2022 standards, and would also increase confidence in the reliability, and ultimately validity, of the outcome measures. Additionally, researchers should ensure that a minimum of 20% IOA data collection occurs for both target and generalization data. That is, generalization data collection should be treated as a separate dependent variable even if it is the same dependent variable in a different setting (e.g., activities) or across different people (e.g., children). This will help ensure that data across all phases are reliably recorded and both target and generalization data are measured accurately.

Systematically manipulating the independent variable. Surprisingly, one of the most common design elements that resulted in studies not meeting 2022 or 2020 standards was regarding researchers systematically introducing the independent variable (i.e., consultation or coaching). Researchers making data-based decisions on visual analysis of data is one of the hallmarks of SCD research (Ledford & Gast, 2018). This criterion was frequently unmet when data were not staggered, which is typical in multiple baseline and probe designs. Additionally, this criterion was unmet when an independent variable was introduced based on collecting a predetermined number of data points versus utilizing visual analysis to determine phase changes. In one instance, a research study simply did not indicate how phase changes were made. As such, we offer the following recommendations.

First, if using a multiple baseline or probe design (which is logically most common for indirect service delivery research), ensure that data are always collected in a staggered manner, with at least a two data point stagger between baseline tiers. Further, if utilizing a concurrent design, the independent variable should only be introduced in the second tier when a treatment effect is visually observed in the first tier (this consideration does not apply to nonconcurrent designs; Ledford & Gast, 2018). However, we acknowledge that sometimes in applied research it is not practical to wait for an ideal level, trend, or stability to implement an independent variable, as this may unnecessarily lengthen the amount of time in which participants (e.g., early childhood educator and their students) receive services/treatment. As such, researchers may consider establishing a predetermined criterion to initiate a phase change (e.g., Johnson et al., 2023; LaBrot et al., 2022; Marsicano et al., 2015).

Additionally, early education indirect service delivery researchers should always describe the manner in which phase change decisions were made. This will not only allow them to meet WWC standards but also will make their research more replicable. Finally, the 2022 WWC standards offer a caveat of implementing the independent variable if the first baseline phase contains zero variability. While this was described as a broad standard for SCD, it does not necessarily consider the collection of generalization data. If early educator generalization of outcomes is a primary research question, we recommend only implementing an independent variable if both the target and generalization data both have zero variability. This will allow for much stronger conclusions about functional relationships between an indirect service delivery practice and early childhood educators' generalized outcomes.

Collecting an adequate amount of data. The most common design standard not met across both the 2022 and 2020 standards was collecting an adequate amount of data per phase. In general, three data points per phase is the minimum criterion for establishing a trend (Cooper et al., 2020; Ledford & Gast, 2018). Even so, three data points would not be sufficient for either the 2022 or 2020 standards. The 2020 standards proposed a minimum of five data points per phase (WWC, 2020) with the 2022 standards retaining this, with the exception of a minimum of six data points per baseline phase (WWC, 2022). The rationale for five data points is that of demonstrating a stable trend as opposed to assuming the first identified trend after only three data points (WWC, 2020, 2022). Despite these standards, considerations for treating generalization data as its own dependent variable are not discussed. So, we recommend two courses of action that are dependent upon whether researchers are probing for generalization (i.e., less data collection than the target variable) or continuously collecting generalization data (i.e., collecting data as often as the target variable).

If probing for generalization, we recommend collecting a minimum of six data points per baseline phase with a minimum of five data points for subsequent phases for target data only. A minimum of three generalization data points per phase should be collected in conjunction with these target data. This would allow for an adequate number of data points and systematic manipulation of the independent variable, and offer information regarding basic level, trend, and variability for generalization data. However, if generalization data are collected continuously (i.e., not probed), then both target and generalization data points should contain the minimum of data points (i.e., six baseline, five for subsequent phases) to meet the 2022 standards. If both target and generalization data are collected continuously, we recommend that phase change decisions be based upon either the target or generalization outcome (not both). This should be predetermined and related to the primary research questions of a given study.

That is, if more interest is in a target variable and generalization is a secondary variable, then target variable data should serve to guide phase change decisions. Conversely, if generalization is of primary importance, then it should serve to inform phase change decisions. Level, trend, and stability of both variables can both be considered to inform phase changes, but this is not recommended if working with a consultee and classroom that require immediate attention (e.g., working with severe behaviors, or with teachers experiencing severe burnout and on the verge of turnover).

Limiting risk of bias. Finally, risk of bias with multiple baseline and probe designs refers to the extent to which there is overlap between phases or baseline data trending in the direction of expected outcomes. We realize it can be tempting to implement an independent variable, such as coaching or consultation, after the recommended minimum number of data points are reached. This is especially challenging in applied research in which participants may be actual consultees awaiting intervention and support. Given the implications of this study's findings and the nature of applied research which is to establish a functional relationship between an independent variable and dependent variable, we strongly urge caution in adopting this practice. Instead, SCD research should continue to collect data until stabilization or a clear trend in the opposite expected direction of the independent variable is established. This should be applied for both target and generalization data. Even if generalization data are probed versus continuously collected, a stable baseline or relevant trend should be established to identify a true functional relationship.

References

*indicates studies included in review

Allday, R. A., Hinkson-Lee, K., Hudson, T., Neilsen-Gatti, S., Kleinke, A., & Russel, C. S. (2012). Training general educators to increase behavior-specific praise: Effects on students with EBD. *Behavioral Disorders, 37*(2), 87-98. https://www.jstor.org/stable/23890733

Barlow, D. H., & Hayes, S. C. (1979). Alternating treatments design: One strategy for comparing the effects of two treatments in a single subject. *Journal of Applied Behavior Analysis, 12*(2), 199-210. doi: 10.1901/jaba.1979.12-199

*Barton, E. E., Pokorski, E. A., Gossett, S., Sweeney, E., Qiu, J., & Choi, G. (2018). The use of email to coach early childhood teachers. *Journal of Early Intervention, 40*(3), 212–228. https://doi.org/10.1177/1053815118760314

Bicer, A. (2021). A systematic literature review: Discipline-specific and general instructional practices fostering the mathematical creativity of students. *International Journal of Education in Mathematics, Science, and Technology (IJEMST), 9*(2), 252-281. https://doi.org/10.46328/ijemst.1254

*Bose-Deakins, J E. (2005). *Increasing early literacy instruction of Head Start teachers using videotape consultation* (Publication No. 3199456) [Doctoral dissertation, The University of Memphis]. ProQuest Dissertations Publishing.

Brock, M. E., Seaman, R. L., & Gatsch, A. L. (2018). Efficacy of video modeling and brief coaching on teacher implementation of an evidence-based practice for students with severe disabilities. *Journal of Special Education Technology, 33*(4), 259-269.

Cole, C.L., Marder, T., & McCann, L. (2000) Self-monitoring. In E.S. Shapiro & T.R. Kratochwill (Eds.). *Conducting school-based assessments of child and adolescent behavior* (pp. 121-149). Guilford Press.

Collier-Meek, M. A., Fallon, L. M., & Gould, K. (2018). How are treatment integrity data assessed? Reviewing the performance feedback literature. *School Psychology Quarterly, 33*(4), 517. https://doi.org/10.1037/spq0000239

*Coogle, C. G., Ottley, J. R., Storie, S., Rahn, N. L., & Kurowski-Burt, A. (2020). Performance-based feedback to enhance preservice teachers' practice and preschool children's expressive communication. *Journal of Teacher Education, 71*(2), 188–202. https://doi.org/10.1177/0022487118803583

*Coogle, C. G., Rahn, N. L., & Ottley, J. R. (2015). Pre-service teacher use of communication strategies upon receiving immediate feedback. *Early Childhood Research Quarterly, 32*, 105–115. https://doi.org/10.1016/j.ecresq.2015.03.003

Cooper, J. O., Heron, T. E., & Heward, W. L. (2020). *Applied Behavior Analysis*. Pearson UK.

Cornelius, K. E., & Nagro, S. A. (2014). Evaluating the evidence base of performance feedback in preservice special education teacher training. *Teacher Education and Special Education, 37*(2), 133-146.

*Crawford, R. V. (2018). *Training teachers to implement systematic strategies in preschool classrooms with fidelity* (dissertation) [University of Kentucky Libraries]. https://doi.org/10.13023/ETD.2018.245

Dong, X., Sanchez, L., Burke, M. D., & Bowman-Perrott, L. (2023). Evidence from single case research on social skills interventions for preschoolers at-risk for EBD: A scoping review and application of quality indicators. *Psychology in the Schools, 60*(7), 2270–2295. https://doi.org/10.1002/pits.22855

*Duncan, N. G., Dufrene, B. A., Sterling, H. E., & Tingstrom, D. H. (2013). Promoting teachers' generalization of intervention use through goal setting and performance feedback. *Journal of Behavioral Education, 22*(4), 325–347. https://doi.org/10.1007/s10864-013-9173-5

Erchul, W. P. (2023). As we coach, so shall we consult: A perspective on coaching research in education. *Journal of School Psychology, 96*, 88–94. https://doi.org/10.1016/j.jsp.2022.10.004

Every Student Succeeds Act, 20 U.S.C. § 6301 (2015).

Fallon, L. M., Collier-Meek, M. A., Maggin, D. M., Sanetti, L. M. H., & Johnson, A. H. (2015). Is performance feedback for educators an evidence-based practice? A systematic review and evaluation based on single-case research. *Exceptional Children, 81*(2), 227–246. https://doi.org/10.1177/0014402914551738

Fallon, L. M., Kurtz, K. D., & Mueller, M. R. (2018). Direct training to improve educators' treatment integrity: A systematic review of single-case design studies. *School Psychology Quarterly, 33*(2), 169. https://doi.org/10.1037/spq0000210

Flower, A., McKenna, J. W., & Haring, C. D. (2017). Behavior and classroom management: Are teacher preparation programs really preparing our teachers? *Preventing School Failure: Alternative Education for Children and Youth, 61*(2), 163–169. https://doi.org/10.1080/1045988X.2016.1231109

*Frantz, R. J. (2017). *Coaching teaching assistants to implement naturalistic behavioral teaching strategies to enhance social communication skills during play in the preschool classroom* (Order no. 10617079). Available from ProQuest Dissertations & Theses Global. (1967146015). http://lynx.lib.usm.edu/dissertations-theses/coaching-teaching-assistants-implement/docview/1967146015/se-2

*Freeland, J. T. (2002). *Analyzing the effects of direct behavioral consultation on teachers: Generalization of skills across settings* (Order No. 3069330). Available from ProQuest Dissertations & Theses Global. (305573307). http://lynx.lib.usm.edu/dissertations-theses/analyzing-effects-direct-behavioral-consultation/docview/305573307/se-2

Freeman, E., Wertheim, E. H., & Trinder, M. (2014). Teacher perspectives on factors facilitating implementation of whole school approaches for resolving conflict. *British Educational Research Journal, 40*(5), 847–868. https://doi.org/10.1002/berj.3116

*Fullerton, E. K., Conroy, M. A., & Correa, V. I. (2009). Early childhood teachers' use of specific praise statements with young children at risk for behavioral disorders. *Behavioral Disorders, 34*(3), 118–135. https://doi.org/10.1177/019874290903400302

*Gouvousis, Aphroditi. (January 2011). *Teacher implemented pivotal response training to improve communication in children with autism spectrum disorders* (Doctoral Dissertation, East Carolina University). Retrieved from the Scholarship. (http://hdl.handle.net/10342/3564.)

Güder, S. Y., Alabay, E., & Güner, E. (2018). Behavioral problems preschool teachers experience in their classrooms and the strategies they employ for these behaviors. *Elementary Education Online, 17*(1).

*Hall, L.J., Grundon, G.S., Pope, C., & Romero, A. (2010). Training paraprofessionals to use behavioral strategies when educating learners with autism spectrum disorders across environments. *Behavioral Interventions, 25*, 37-51.

*Hemmeter, M. L., Hardy, J. K., Schnitz, A. G., Adams, J. M., & Kinder, K. A. (2015). Effects of training and coaching with performance feedback on teachers' use of *Pyramid Model* practices. *Topics in Early Childhood Special Education, 35*(3), 144–156. https://doi.org/10.1177/0271121415594924

*Hundert, J. P. (2007). Training classroom and resource preschool teachers to develop inclusive class interventions for children with disabilities: Generalization to new intervention targets. *Journal of Positive Behavior Interventions, 9*(3), 159-173. https://doi-org.lynx.lib.usm.edu/10.1177/10983007070090030401

Johnson, C. N., Cato, T. A., LaBrot, Z. C., & DeFouw, E. R. (2023). Evaluation of emailed prompts to promote generalization and maintenance of preschool teachers' effective instruction delivery. *Behavioral Interventions, 39* (1), e1973. https://doi.org/10.1002/bin.1973

*Kaiser, A. P., Ostrosky, M. M., & Alpert, C. L. (1993). Training teachers to use environmental arrangement and milieu teaching with nonvocal preschool children. *Journal of the Association for Persons with Severe Handicaps, 18*(3), 188-199. https://doi-org.lynx.lib.usm.edu/10.1177/154079699301800305

Kirkpatrick, M., Akers, J., & Rivera, G. (2019). Use of behavioral skills training with teachers: A systematic review. *Journal of Behavioral Education, 28*, 344-361.

Kratochwill, T. R., Hitchcock, J., Horner, R. H., Levin, J. R., Odom, S. L., Rindskopf, D. M., & Shadish, W. R. (2010). Single-case designs technical documentation. *What works clearinghouse.*

Kratochwill, T. R., & Levin, J. R. (2010). Enhancing the scientific credibility of single-case intervention research: Randomization to the rescue. *Psychological Methods, 15*(2), 124-144.

*LaBrot, Z. C., Dufrene, B. A., Olmi, D. J., Dart, E. H., Radley, K., Lown, E., & Pasqua, J. L. (2020). Maintenance and generalization of preschool teachers' use of behavior-specific praise following in situ training. *Journal of Behavioral Education, 30*(3), 350–377. https://doi.org/10.1007/s10864-020-09375-5

LaBrot, Z. C., Pasqua, J. L., Dufrene, B. A., Brewer, E. A., & Goff, B. (2016). In situ training for increasing head start after-care teachers' use of praise. *Journal of Behavioral Education, 25*, 32-48.

LaBrot, Z. C., Smith, T. E., Maxime, E., & Lawson, A. (in press). School-based consultation and coaching for promoting teachers' generalized outcomes: A meta-analysis. *Journal of School Psychology.*

LaBrot, Z. C., Weaver, C., Peak, L., Maxime, E., Butt, S., Johnson, C., Pigg, B., & Hamilton, F. (2022). Multitiered consultation to promote preservice teachers' delivery of behavior-specific praise in early childhood education classrooms. *Journal of Behavioral Education.*

Ledford, J. R., & Gast, D. L. (2018). *Single case research methodology: Applications in special education and behavioral sciences.* (3rd ed.). Routledge.

*Lerman, D. C., Vorndran, C. M., Addison, L., & Kuhn, S. C. (2004). Preparing teachers in evidence-based practices for young children with autism. *School Psychology Review, 33*(4), 510–526. https://doi.org/10.1080/02796015.2004.12086265

Long, A. C., Hagermoser Sanetti, L. M., Collier-Meek, M. A., Gallucci, J., Altschaefl, M., & Kratochwill, T. R. (2016). An exploratory investigation of teachers' intervention planning and perceived implementation barriers. *Journal of School Psychology, 55,* 1–26. https://doi.org/10.1016/j.jsp.2015.12.002

Love, J. M. (2010). Effects of Early Head Start prior to kindergarten entry: The importance of early experience. Society for Research on Educational Effectiveness. https://eric.ed.gov/?id=ED514662

*Lynes, M. J. (2012). *The effects of self-evaluation with video on the use of oral language development strategies by preschool teachers* (Order No. 3505030). Available from ProQuest Dissertations & Theses Global. (1012121473). http://lynx.lib.usm.edu/dissertations-theses/effects-self-evaluation-with-video-on-use-oral/docview/1012121473/se-2

*Madigan, R. J. (2011). *Effectiveness of teacher-child interaction training (TCIT): A multiple probe design across classrooms in a day-treatment preschool* (Order no. 3482071). Available from ProQuest Dissertations & Theses Global. (907549187). http://lynx.lib.usm.edu/dissertations-theses/effectiveness-teacher-child-interaction-training/docview/907549187/se-2

Maggin, D. M., Barton, E., Reichow, B., Lane, K. L., & Shogren, K. A. (2022). Commentary on the What Works Clearinghouse Standards and Procedures Handbook (v. 4.1) for the Review of Single-Case Research. *Remedial and Special Education, 43*(6), 421–433. https://doi.org/10.1177/07419325211051317

Maggin, D. M., Briesch, A. M., & Chafouleas, S. M. (2013). An application of the What Works Clearinghouse Standards for Evaluating Single-Subject Research: Synthesis of the self-management literature base. *Remedial and Special Education, 34*(1), 44–58. https://doi.org/10.1177/0741932511435176

Markelz, A., Riden, B., & Scheeler, M. C. (2017). Generalization training in special education teacher preparation: does it exist? *Teacher Education and Special Education: The Journal of the Teacher Education Division of the Council for Exceptional Children, 40*(3), 179–193. https://doi.org/10.1177/0888406417703752

*Marsicano, R. T., Morrison, J. Q., Moomaw, S. C., Fite, N. M., & Kluesener, C. M. (2015). Increasing math milieu teaching by varying levels of consultation support: An example of analyzing intervention strength. *Journal of Behavioral Education, 24*(1), 112–132. https://doi.org/10.1007/s10864-014-9200-1

*Peck, C. A., Killen, C. C., & Baumgart, D. (1989). Increasing implementation of special education instruction in mainstream preschools: Direct and generalized effects of nondirective consultation. *Journal of Applied Behavior Analysis, 22*(2), 197–210. https://doi.org/10.1901/jaba.1989.22-197

*Pellecchia, M., Connell, J. E., Eisenhart, D., Kane, M., Schoener, C., Turkel, K., Riley, M., & Mandell, D. S. (2011). We're all in this together now: Group performance feedback to increase classroom team data collection. *Journal of School Psychology, 49*(4), 411–431. https://doi.org/10.1016/j.jsp.2011.04.003

*Rakap, S. (2017). Impact of coaching on preservice teachers' use of embedded instruction in inclusive preschool classrooms. *Journal of Teacher Education, 68*(2), 125–139. https://doi.org/10.1177/0022487116685753

Reddy, L. A., Barboza-Whitehead, S., Files, T., & Reddy, L. A. (2000). Clinical focus of consultation outcome research with children and adolescents. *Special Services in the Schools, 16*(1–2), 1–22. https://doi.org/10.1300/J008v16n01_01

Reinke, W. M., Stormont, M., Herman, K. C., Puri, R., & Goel, N. (2011). Supporting children's mental health in schools: Teacher perceptions of needs, roles, and barriers. *School Psychology Quarterly, 26*(1), 1–13. https://doi.org/10.1037/a0022714

Robinson, V., & Swanton, C. (1980). The generalization of behavioral teacher training. *Review of Educational Research, 50*(3), 486–498. https://doi.org/10.3102/00346543050003486

Schaack, D. D., Le, V.-N., & Stedron, J. (2020). When fulfillment is not enough: Early childhood teacher occupational burnout and turnover intentions from a job demands and resources perspective. *Early Education and Development, 31*(7), 1011–1030. https://doi.org/10.1080/10409289.2020.1791648

Scheeler, M. C., Bruno, K., Grubb, E., & Seavey, T. L. (2009). Generalizing teaching techniques from university to k-12 classrooms: Teaching preservice teachers to use what they learn. *Journal of Behavioral Education, 18*(3), 189–210. https://doi.org/10.1007/s10864-009-9088-3

Shapiro, E. S., Kazdin, A. E., & McGonigle, J. J. (1982). Multiple-treatment interference in the simultaneous- or alternating-treatments design. *Behavioral Assessment, 4*(1), 105–115.

*Shepley, C. N. (2019). *Training teachers in inclusive preschool classrooms to monitor child progress and make data-based decisions through direct behavioral observation* [Doctoral dissertation, University of Kentucky Libraries]. https://doi.org/10.13023/ETD.2019.068

Smith, T. E., Holmes, S. R., Sheridan, S. M., Cooper, J. M., Bloomfield, B. S., & Preast, J. L. (2021). The effects of consultation-based family-school engagement on student and parent outcomes: a meta-analysis. *Journal of Educational and Psychological Consultation*, *31*(3), 278–306. https://doi.org/10.1080/10474412.2020.1749062

Smith, T. E., LaBrot, Z. C., Maxime, E., & Lawson, A. (2023). School-based consultation to promote generalization of early childhood educators' evidence-based practices: A meta-analysis. *Perspectives on Early Childhood Psychology and Education*, *7*(2). https://doi.org/10.58948/2834-8257.1023

Snell, M. E., Berlin, R. A., Voorhees, M. D., Stanton-Chapman, T. L., & Hadden, S. (2012). A survey of preschool staff concerning problem behavior and its prevention in Head Start classrooms. *Journal of Positive Behavior Interventions*, *14*(2), 98–107. https://doi.org/10.1177/1098300711416818

Stokes, T. F., & Baer, D. M. (1977). An implicit technology of generalization. *Journal of Applied Behavior Analysis*, *10*(2), 349–367. https://doi.org/10.1901/jaba.1977.10-349

Stormont, M., Reinke, W. M., Newcomer, L., Marchese, D., & Lewis, C. (2015). Coaching teachers' use of social behavior interventions to improve children's outcomes: A review of the literature. *Journal of Positive Behavior Interventions*, *17*(2), 69–82. https://doi.org/10.1177/1098300714550657

U.S. Bureau of Labor Statistics. (2023). *Occupational outlook handbook. What preschool teachers do.* Retrieved from https://www.bls.gov/ooh/education-training-and-library/preschool-teachers.htm#tab-2

*Van Vonderen, A., Duker, P., & Didden, R. (2010). Professional development improves staff's implementation of rehabilitation programmes for children with severe-to-profound intellectual disability. *Developmental Neurorehabilitation*, *13*(5), 351–359. https://doi.org/10.3109/17518423.2010.493916

Wahman, C. L., Pustejovsky, J. E., Ostrosky, M. M., & Santos, R. M. (2022). Examining the effects of social stories on challenging behavior and prosocial skills in young children: A systematic review and meta-analysis. *Topics In Early Childhood Education*, *41*(4), 267-279.

*Watkins-Emonet, C. (2000). *Evaluating the teaching components of Direct Behavioral Consultation on skill acquisition and generalization in Head Start classrooms* (Order No. 9991331). Available from ProQuest Dissertations & Theses Global. (304608519). http://lynx.lib.usm.edu/dissertations-theses/evaluating-teaching-components-direct-behavioral/docview/304608519/se-2

Weiland, C., Ulvestad, K., Sachs, J., & Yoshikawa, H. (2013). Associations between classroom quality and children's vocabulary and executive function skills in an urban public prekindergarten program. *Early Childhood Research Quarterly*, *28*(2), 199–209. https://doi.org/10.1016/j.ecresq.2012.12.002

What Works Clearinghouse. (2020). *What Works Clearinghouse standards handbook*, version 4.1. Washington, DC: U.S. Department of Education, Institute of Education Sciences, National Center for Education Evaluation and Regional Assistance. https://ies.ed.gov/ncee/wwc/handbooks.

What Works Clearinghouse. (2022). *What Works Clearinghouse procedures and standards handbook*, version 5.0. U.S. Department of Education, Institute of Education Sciences, National Center for Education Evaluation and Regional Assistance (NCEE). https://ies.ed.gov/ncee/wwc/Handbooks.

*Wimberly, J.K. (2016). *Generalization of teachers' use of effective instruction delivery following in situ training*. (Publication no. 269) [Master's Thesis, University of Southern Mississippi]. 269. https://aquila.usm.edu/masters_theses/269

Using Effect Sizes, Confidence Intervals, and the Bayes Factor to Better Understand the t-test, Analysis of Variance, and Regression Results

W. Holmes Finch

Abstract

Null hypothesis testing is a widely used paradigm for assessing research hypotheses across the social sciences. Despite their ubiquity, researchers have discussed a number of problems and limitations to hypothesis testing and have suggested alternatives that might provide greater depth and explanation of research results. The purpose of this paper is to describe the use of several such alternatives, and to show how they can be integrated with one another and with null hypothesis testing in order to provide a more holistic view of research hypotheses.

Perhaps the most common statistical analyses used in the social sciences derive from the general linear model. Underneath this model lie methods such as the *t*-test, analysis of variance (ANOVA), and linear regression. These techniques can be found throughout the social science literature (Djonko-Moore, 2022; Schachter et al., 2016; Wright, 2006). Traditionally, the focus of descriptions of these analyses lies on hypothesis test results. These tests assess a null hypothesis, which typically states that there is no effect in the population, where an effect might be group mean differences or relationships between two variables. For example, the null hypothesis for a 2-sample *t*-test states that the mean of a dependent variable is not different between two groups in the population. In the context of regression, the most common null hypothesis is that the slope relating an independent variable (*x*) and a dependent variable (*y*) is equal to 0 in the population. The null hypothesis testing procedure produces a test statistic and its associated *p*-value that is used to assess the null hypothesis. When the *p*-value is less than a predetermined threshold, called a, the researcher would reject the null hypothesis. Most commonly, a is set at 0.05, so that when $p \leq 0.05$, the researcher will reject the null.

Despite its popularity and widespread use, null hypothesis testing is not without its limitations. Authors have criticized it for being too narrowly focused on simple differences, without regard to the size of those differences (Gliner, et al., 2002). In addition, it is quite often limited to use with a very narrow hypothesis about the population, ignoring a much wider array of possible scenarios (Haig, 2017). And the overuse of null hypothesis testing has been associated with the replication crisis in psychology and other social sciences (Colling & Szucs, 2021). Given these concerns, it has been suggested that researchers make use of alternative statistical techniques to support the use of traditional hypothesis testing (Wilcox & Serang, 2017). The purpose of this manuscript is to describe how researchers can incorporate some of these alternatives to null hypothesis testing, including effect sizes, confidence intervals, the Bayes Factor, and dominance analysis into their research. The addition of these methods, in conjunction with standard null hypothesis testing, can provide the researcher with a more complete picture of a population. In the following sections, we will briefly review the technical details of effect sizes used in conjunction with the t-test, analysis of variance (ANOVA), and regression, the Bayes Factor, and dominance analysis, which is used with regression. We will then work through a set of examples demonstrating how these techniques can be used along with hypothesis testing, and then finish by discussing implications for practice.

Effect sizes

As discussed above, by themselves, hypothesis testing results only tell us about the likelihood that the sample we have comes from the population characterized by the null hypothesis. As an example using the logic of null hypothesis testing described above, if the *p*-value for a *t*-test comparing two groups' means is 0.01, we would reject the null hypothesis of no difference and conclude that it is unlikely our sample came from the population in which the groups had equivalent means for the dependent variable. Although hypothesis tests can be very useful tools, they do not provide us with any information about the size of the difference between the means, in this example. Therefore, in order to better understand the nature and importance of the effects in our sample, we need to investigate its magnitude. Collectively, statistics designed to reflect the magnitude of these effects are referred to as effect sizes. Most commonly used statistical analyses have an associated effect size. Although differing in terms of how they are calculated and what aspects of the effects they highlight, all effect sizes are used with the common goal of describing how large the effects in the sample are, as a way of better understanding their importance. We will focus on three effect size statistics, each of which is associated with a widely used statistical analysis, including the independent samples t-test, ANOVA, and linear regression. One caveat to keep in mind when using effect sizes is that they tend to become more variable in value as sample sizes decrease (Slavin & Smith, 2009). Researchers should keep this fact in mind as they interpret their effect size estimates.

If our primary interest is in comparing means of a dependent variable for two groups, we are most likely to use Cohen's d. This statistic is calculated as:

$$d = \frac{(x_1 - x_2)}{s_p} \tag{1}$$

Where

x_1 = Mean for group 1

x_2 = Mean for group 2

s_p = Standard deviation of the dependent variable pooled across the two groups

Larger values of d reflect a larger standardized difference between the groups' means, in terms of standard deviations. For example, a value of 0.5 would be interpreted as a group mean difference of one half of a standard deviation. There are not hard and fast rules about what value of d connotes a large or a small effect. Cohen (1988) suggested some guidelines for interpreting d that are commonly used in practice. However, these guidelines are not intended to taken as absolute (Cohen), and researchers should always consider the values they obtain for their data in light of the literature in their field. With that caveat in mind, Cohen's guidelines for interpreting d are:

$0.2 \leq d < 0.5$: Small

$0.5 \leq d < 0.8$: Medium

$0.8 < d$: Large

When comparing more than two groups' means using ANOVA, a commonly used effect size is ω^2, which reflects the proportion of variability in the dependent variable that is associated with group membership. Thus, higher values reflect a greater proportion of variability in the dependent variable that the researcher can understand by knowing an individual's group membership. As with d, there are some loose guidelines for interpreting the magnitude of ω^2 that can be used to help researchers understand their results, but which should be used with care. Field (2013) suggested the following guidelines for interpreting ω^2:

$0.01 \leq \omega^2 < 0.06$: Small

$0.06 \leq \omega^2 < 0.14$: Medium

$0.14 < \omega^2$: Large

Cohen's (1992) guidelines are:

$0.02 \leq \omega^2 < 0.13$: Small

$0.13 \leq \omega^2 < 0.26$: Medium

$0.26 < \omega^2$: Large

There are not current recommendations for which of these

guidelines researchers should use in practice. Thus, it might be best to consider our values of ω^2 in light of both sets of guidelines and then couch our conclusions in that light.

Certainly the most commonly used measure of effects for regression is R^2, which reflects the proportion of variance in the dependent variable that is associated with the set of independent variables. In this regard R^2, is very similar to ω^2 in terms of how it quantifies the relationships present in the data. Larger values of R^2 suggest that when a researcher knows the values for the set of independent variables, they will be better able to predict values of the dependent variable. Cohen (1988) suggested the following guidelines for interpreting R^2:

$0.02 \leq R^2 < 0.13$: Small

$0.13 \leq R^2 < 0.26$: Medium

$0.26 < R^2$: Large

The reader will note that these guidelines are equivalent to those Cohen gave for ω^2, reflecting the fact that they provide essentially equivalent measures of the effect in question.

Confidence intervals

Confidence intervals are useful tools that communicate the amount of sampling variability in the data by reflecting the likely range of potential values for the parameter(s) of interest. These intervals are described in terms of the likelihood that the population parameter lies within the range of values. For example, if the 95% confidence interval for the mean score of a standardized test given to 2nd grade students is 25.3 to 34.9, we can be fairly confident (95% confident, in fact) that the population mean lies between these two values. Confidence intervals can be calculated for other parameters, such as the difference between group means or regression slopes. They are, therefore, quite useful tools for researchers to include in their description of statistical results.

Bayes Factor

In addition to effect sizes and hypothesis testing, the Bayes Factor (BF) can be a useful tool for comparing the likelihood of two hypotheses about the data being true in the population (Gu, 2022; Gu et al., 2021). For example, let's consider two hypotheses that might be associated with an ANOVA used to compare means for three groups. Furthermore, we will assume that prior literature and research leads us to believe that the following two hypotheses are most likely to be true for the population:

$$H_1: \mu_1 > \mu_2 > \mu_3 \qquad (2)$$
$$H_2: \mu_2 > \mu_1 > \mu_3$$

The first hypothesis states that the mean for group 1 is larger than that of group 2, which is larger than that of group 3. The second hypothesis states that group 2 has a larger mean than group 1 with group 3 having the smallest mean value. The results of an ANOVA would only be able to test the null hypothesis

$$H_\theta: \mu_1 > \mu_2 > \mu_3 \qquad (3)$$

Follow-up tests, such as Tukey's pairwise comparisons procedure would then test specific group mean differences (e.g., $H_\theta: \mu_1 = \mu_2$). While potentially useful for determining group mean differences, this hypothesis test based approach will not provide us with much direct information about the likelihoods of the two hypotheses that the literature has suggested might hold in the population. It is for addressing this question that the BF can be quite useful.

The BF compares the marginal likelihood associated with each of two hypotheses. Marginal likelihoods are simply the probability of a specific hypothesis given the data at hand (Gu et al., 2021). The BF is calculated as

$$BF_{ia} = \frac{f_i}{c_i} \qquad (4)$$

Where

f_i = Fit of H_1

c_i = Complexity of H_1

The fit of hypothesis H_1 refers to how well the hypothesis conforms to patterns seen in the data, with larger values indicating a closer match. In Bayesian modeling terms, this proximity of the hypothesis to the data (f_i) is referred to as the posterior density of the data. Put another way, the posterior density reflects where the estimates from the Bayesian procedure lie. The denominator of the BF, c_i, is a number assessing the complexity of the hypothesis. More informative hypotheses (i.e., those that make more detailed statements about the population) have higher levels of complexity. In Bayesian terms, c_i is the prior density of H_1. The prior density simply reflects where the prior distribution values lay. Thus, the BF for a hypothesis is the ratio of how closely it conforms to the observed data divided by its specificity. Larger values of the BF for a hypothesis mean that the hypothesis is more likely to hold in the population.

Two likelihoods of competing hypotheses, such as in our example above, can be compared to one another using a ratio of their BFs (Gu et al., 2018):

$$BF_{ii'} = \frac{BF_{ia}}{BF_{i'a}} \qquad (5)$$

Where

BF_{ia} = BF for H_1

$BF_{i'a}$ = BF for $H_{1i'}$

Thus, in order to compare H_1 and H_2 above, we would calculate the BF for each and then take their ratio as

$$BF_{12} = \frac{BF_1}{BF_2} \qquad (6)$$

One standard used by many researchers to identify support of one hypothesis over another is a BF of 3 or more (Kaplan, 2014). Thus, values of this statistic between 1/3 and 3 fall into what is termed the region of indecision, meaning that it is not possible to say that one hypothesis definitively fits with the data better than the other. In addition to the BF, inference can also involve interpretation of the posterior probabilities associated with each hypothesis. The posterior probability reflects the likelihood of an individual hypothesis holding in the population, given the data at hand. Hypotheses with larger posterior probabilities are considered more likely than those with lower probabilities. These posterior probabilities can be used to select from among the considered hypotheses.

Dominance analysis for observed variable models

Researchers interested in gaining insights into the relative importance of predictor variables in multiple regression with respect to an outcome might use dominance analysis (DA; Azen & Budescu, 2003). The overarching goal of DA is to rank order the predictors in terms of the amount of variance in the dependent variable that each explains, based on values of R^2. More specifically, DA involves the calculation of ΔR_j^2, which is the change in variance explained when independent variable j is in the model versus when it is removed. For example, in order to ascertain whether variable j is relatively more important than variable l, with respect to the dependent variable, every possible subset of the remaining k independent variables is used in regression analysis. For each of these subsets, a model without either variables k or l is fit and the R^2 value is retained. Then a model involving this variable subset, as well as variable j is fit to the data and the resulting R^2 is saved. Finally, a model involving the original variable subset, also including variable k, is fit to the data and the R^2 value is retained. The change in R^2 for each variable is then calculated (i.e., ΔR_j^2 and ΔR_l^2). This approach is applied to all possible subsets and variable combinations possible for a given dataset.

There are three types of dominance possible in the context of DA:
1. Complete dominance occurs when ΔR^2 is always larger for variable j than variable l for all possible model subsets.
2. Conditional dominance occurs when for any size of subset model, the mean ΔR^2 for variable j is greater than that of variable l. But this doesn't mean that for each model, ΔR^2 is larger for variable 1.
3. General dominance occurs when across all possible models the average ΔR^2 for variable j is larger than that of variable l.
4. General dominance is perhaps the most widely used in practice (Azen & Budescu, 2003; Azen & Traxel, 2009), and is calculated as

$$d_j = \frac{1}{J} \sum(j-1) \frac{1}{C(J-1,m)} \sum C(J-1,m) \, R^2_{x_j} \mid S_{qm}(x_j) \quad (7)$$
$$\qquad\qquad\qquad m=0$$

Where

m = Size of model prior to entry of x_j

$C(J-1,m)$ = Number of combinations when selecting m elements from $J-1$ possibilities

$S_{qm}(x_j)$ = Subset of variables to which can be added, given m

$R^2_{x_j} \mid S_{qm}(x_j)$ = Squared semipartial correlation of the dependent variable d_j and given $S_{qm}(x_j)$

The statistic d_j is the average increase in the variance accounted for by variable j after the variance explained by other variables in the model is accounted for ($R^2_{x_j} \mid S_{qm}(x_j)$) for variable x_j, across all independent variable subsets. Independent variables with larger values of d_j are said to exhibit general dominance over those variables with smaller values.

It is tempting to use the standardized coefficients (Beta weights) to make such comparisons, given that they represent standardized relationships between the individual independent variables and the response. However, researchers have shown that because the beta weight for a given independent variable includes shared variance with other variables in the model, they are not particularly useful for determining variable importance (Pedhazur, 1997; Capraro & Capraro, 2001; LeBreton et al., 2004). Therefore, it is generally not recommended for the purpose of ordering independent variables in terms of their relationship with the dependent variable.

One approach to inference that has been suggested for DA involves the bootstrap, which accounts for the sampling variability inherent in these values (e.g., Braun et al., 2019; Azen & Budescu, 2003; Azen & Traxel, 2009; Tonidandel et al., 2009;). In statistics, bootstrapping involves resampling individuals within the original sample with replacement and then running the desired analysis on this new sample. This process is repeated a large d_j number of times (e.g., 1000) and the resulting statistics, such as are saved. In the context of DA, for each of these bootstrap samples, the ordering of the variables based on d_j is ascertained. These values can then be summarized in order to obtain the probability of various variable orderings once sampling variability has been taken into account. In this way, we can gain insights into what may be the most likely ordering variables in terms of their importance, after accounting for the fact that our sample is only one of an infinite number that could come from the population.

Independent samples t-test example

We will first consider a relatively simple data analysis scenario in which the researcher is interested in comparing means between two groups. All data analyses in this manuscript were carried out using the R software package (R Core Team, 2023). In this case, we will compare the mean reading test scores between a sample of 15 2nd-grade female and male students. The test has a minimum possible score of 0 and a maximum of 10 points. The mean and standard deviation for the sample appear in Table 1. For this sample, the female students had a larger mean than did the males. However, sample values alone cannot be used to make determinations regarding differences in the population. Therefore, we will need to use an inferential statistical method, such as the t-test, to compare the means from the sample, in order to gain insights into whether male and female students are likely to have different reading test performance in the broader population.

Table 1
Descriptive statistics for t-test example

Group	N	Mean	Standard Devation
Female	15	7.87	1.36
Male	15	7.51	1.40

Prior to conducting the t-test, we need to assess assumptions that underlie the procedure, including equality of group variances and normality of the scores. The variances in reading test scores for males and females can be compared using a F-test, where the null hypothesis is that the groups' variances are equal. For this sample, the p-value of the test was 0.9102, meaning that we do not reject the null and thus conclude that the reading test variances are equal for the female and male students. We can assess the normality of the reading test scores using the QQ plot, which graphs the data along with a line showing where the data would be expected to lie if it were normally distributed. This graph appears in Figure 1, along with lines for a confidence interval for normality. If the data points for the raw data lie within the interval, we can conclude that it is likely to be normally distributed in the population. The results in Figure 1 suggest that the data is indeed likely to be normally distributed, given that the bulk of points fall within the 95% confidence interval around the normal line.

Given that we have established the homogeneity of group variances and normality of the score, we can now conduct the t-test comparing the reading score means between the male and female students. The null hypothesis of this test is that the means are equal

Figure 1
QQ Plot for reading test scores

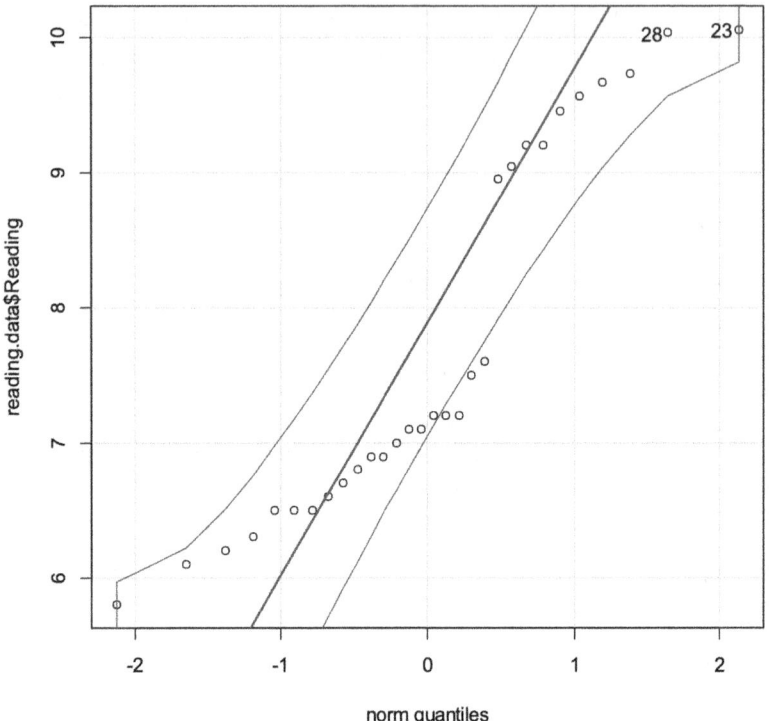

to one another and our alternative hypothesis is that they are not equal. The value of the *t* was -0.708 with 28 degrees of freedom, yielding a *p*-value of 0.4846. Because *p* is not less than 0.05 (our alpha level), we would not reject the null hypothesis that the reading test means are equal for females and males. In addition to the *t*-test, we can also examine the 95% confidence interval for the group mean differences, which reflects the range of values within which we can be fairly certain the actual difference lies. For this example, the confidence interval ranges between -1.39 and 0.68, meaning that it's reasonable to believe that females could have a mean reading test score as much as 1.39 points larger than that of males, or that males could have a mean score 0.68 points larger than that of females. The fact that 0 is contained in the confidence interval means that it is also reasonable to conclude that there is no difference in the group means.

The Cohen's *d* effect size value is -0.26, with a 95% confidence interval of -0.98 to 0.46. This value indicates that the male mean score is approximately ¼ of a standard deviation smaller than that for females, which falls into Cohen's small category (Cohen, 1988). In addition, the fact that 0 lies within this interval provides further evidence that it is unlikely reading test means differ for females and males in the population.

To this point, we have used a traditional approach to examining group mean differences, including the *t*-test and Cohen's *d* effect size. This information is certainly useful for researchers to understand whether there are group differences in the population mean and the magnitude of this difference, based on the effect size. However, we can use some basic information from the Bayesian paradigm (described above) to understand the likelihood of specific hypotheses about the population vis-à-vis one another. Researchers may wish to examine the viability of various hypotheses in cases where there are multiple viable theoretical possibilities for how the groups' means might differ (or not) within the population. The standard ANOVA approach allows the researcher to test only a single null hypothesis, whereas the Bayes factor method can accommodate comparisons of multiple hypotheses with one another, representing an extension of the standard hypothesis testing paradigm.

As an example, when comparing the mean reading scores for female and male students, we might consider three possible outcomes: The population means are equal, females have a higher reading test mean in the population, or males have a higher reading test mean in the population. As we discussed earlier, each of these hypotheses has an associated Bayes factor, which reflects the likelihood of the hypothesis versus the likelihood of an unconstrained (noninformative) hypothesis. Essentially, larger Bayes factors reflect a greater likelihood of the hypothesis being true. In addition, using the Bayesian paradigm, we can obtain the probability of each hypothesis being true, given the data at hand.

The Bayes factors and hypothesis probabilities appear in Table 2. From these results, we see that the most likely hypothesis is equal means, with a probability of 0.68. In other words, the probability that in the population male and female students have equal reading test means is 0.68. In contrast, the least likely hypothesis is that the mean male reading test score is greater than that of females. The equal means hypothesis is more than 4 times as likely as the unconstrained hypothesis, given the BF of 4.26. More interestingly, we can calculate the BF for the hypotheses of interest, such as equal means versus females having the higher reading test score: $\frac{0.68}{0.24} = 2.83$. This result means that it is nearly 3 times more likely that the reading test means are equal than that females have a higher mean than do males.

Table 2
Bayes factors and posterior probabilities for hypotheses regarding gender mean reading test differences

Hypothesis	Bayes Factor*	Probability
Equal means	4.26	0.68
Male reading mean is larger than female reading mean	0.48	0.08
Female reading mean is larger than male reading mean	1.52	0.24

Note: *Likelihood of hypothesis compared to unconstrained hypothesis

Now that we have considered several pieces of evidence regarding gender mean differences of the reading test scores for our 2nd grade sample, we can synthesize what we have found. First, it appears to be most likely that the female and male students perform equivalently on the reading assessment. The t-test was not statistically significant, and the most likely hypothesis was of group mean equality. Furthermore, the sample means differed by somewhat less than a fourth of a standard deviation, which falls within Cohen's small range. However, although the most likely case is equal group means, this should not be taken as an absolutely definitive result. The probability of equal means being true is 0.68, which means that there is a probability of 0.32 that some other outcome is the case. The most likely of these, though still not very likely, is that female students perform better on the reading assessment than do the males. In summary, it's most likely that the genders have equal mean test scores, but it is not a certainty. The primary lesson here is that we should not rely solely on the result of a *t*-test, but should also incorporate confidence intervals, effect sizes and Bayes factors to obtain a full picture of the hypotheses of interest to us.

Analysis of variance example

Our next example involves the same data set as we used for the t-test, but now we are interested in comparing the mean reading test scores across three methods of instruction, each of which has 10 randomly assigned students. The three treatment groups were defined as: (1) Group tutoring, (2) Individual tutoring online, and (3) Individual tutoring in-person. We are interested in assessing whether there are population differences in mean reading test scores for the treatments, and whether the population means can be ordered as follows: Individual in-person tutoring > Individual online tutoring > Group tutoring. The means and standard deviations of the reading test scores for the three treatments appear in Table 3. For the sample, we can see that the largest mean test score was associated with the in-person tutoring treatment, and the lowest was associated with group tutoring. However, as we discussed previously, differences in the sample mean cannot be assumed to hold in the population, due to sampling variability. Thus, we will need to use analysis of variance (ANOVA) to compare the group means.

The *F*-test that is at the core of ANOVA, like the *t*-test, rests on the assumptions of homogeneity of variance and normality of the dependent variable. We assessed the normality assumption prior to conducting the *t*-test and found that it held. The homogeneity of variance assumption can be tested using Levene's test, which assesses the null hypothesis that the group variances are equal. For this example, the p-value for Levene's test was 0.6918, meaning that we do not reject the null hypothesis and thereby conclude that the treatments' variances are equal in the population. Thus, we can move forward with the ANOVA.

Table 3
Means and standard deviations for reading test scores by treatment group

Hypothesis	Bayes Factor*	Probability
Group tutoring	6.49	0.42
Online individual tutoring	7.08	0.32
In-person individual tutoring	9.49	0.39

The p-value for the F-test comparing the treatment means across the three methods was less than 0.001, leading us to reject the null hypothesis that the means are equal in the population. Next, we can use a post hoc comparison method, such as Tukey's test, to compare pairs of means in order to determine which groups differ from one another. The results of these comparisons appear in Table 4. These results reveal that there were statistically significant differences between each pair of reading group means. Combining these results with the means in Table 3, we conclude that students receiving in-person tutoring had the highest mean reading scores, followed by the online tutoring group, with the group tutoring students having the lowest test mean.

Table 4
Results for Tukey's mean comparison procedure

Comparison	Difference	Standard error	t	p
Online—Group	0.59	0.17	3.48	0.005
In-person—Group	3.00	0.17	17.70	<0.001
In-person—Online	2.41	0.17	14.23	<0.001

Using Effect Sizes, Confidence Intervals, and the Bayes Factor 59

As was the case for the *t*-test, we would like to characterize our results using an effect size. For ANVOA there are multiple such statistics to choose from, with being perhaps the optimal one to use (Kroes & Finley, 2023). The statistic reflects the proportion of variability in the dependent variable (reading test score) that is associated with the group variable (treatment). For this example, meaning that approximately 92% of the variability in reading test scores in our sample is associated with the type of tutoring that the students received. This finding suggests that the tutoring treatment method had a large impact on reading test performance.

Finally, using the Bayes factors and associated probabilities, we can assess the likelihood of various hypotheses of interest holding in the population. We have four hypotheses of interest:

The first hypothesis is the one tested by the ANOVA and states that treatment doesn't impact reading test score. The second hypothesis states that in-person individual tutoring yields a higher reading mean than online individual tutoring, which in turn yields a higher mean than group tutoring. The third hypothesis states that group and individual online tutoring yield the same mean reading score, with in-person individual tutoring having the highest mean. Finally, the fourth hypothesis indicates that the group tutoring method yields a lower mean reading score, whereas the two in-person tutoring methods produce equal mean reading scores.

The results of the Bayes factor analyses appear in Table 5. It is clear from these results that by far the most likely hypothesis is , in which the group tutoring mean is lower than the online individual mean, which is lower than the in-person individual mean. The probability of this hypothesis is 0.997, meaning that it is highly likely to be true in the population. It is also 5.88 times more likely than the unconstrained hypothesis. No other hypothesis was at all likely, based on the results from this sample. Taken together, the results for comparing reading test means for the tutoring methods reveal that being individually tutored in-person yields the highest reading test scores and group tutoring yields the lowest such means, and this ordering of mean scores is highly likely to be true in the population. In addition, the tutoring method greatly impacts the reading test score and thus should therefore receive much attention from school officials.

Table 5
Bayes factors and posterior probabilities for hypotheses regarding treatment mean reading test differences

Hypothesis	Bayes factor*	Probability
Group = Online = In-person	0	0
Group < Online < In-person	5.88	0.997
Group = Online < In-person	0.02	0.003
Group < Online = In-person	0	0

Note: *Likelihood of hypothesis compared to unconstrained hypothesis

Regression example

Our final example involves using multiple linear regression to examine relationships between a measure of self-oriented perfectionism and four scores measuring achievement motivation: mastery approach, mastery avoidance, performance approach, and performance avoidance. In brief, a high mastery goal orientation score means that an individual is primarily interested in becoming better at a skill or endeavor (e.g., better understanding good pedagogy practice), whereas a high performance goal orientation score indicates that an individual is most interested in outcomes (e.g., being viewed by others as a good teacher). Goal approach orientation refers to a desire to be viewed (by oneself and/or others) positively, and a goal avoidance orientation refers to a desire to not be viewed negatively. A high self-oriented perfectionism score means that the individual is driven by an internal desire for perfection. The data were collected from a sample of 432 elementary school teachers, and the context in which teachers were asked to respond involved their classroom practices. Of primary interest are the relationships between the individual goal orientation scores and self-oriented perfectionism. In addition, we would also like to compare the importance of several variables with one another. Put another way, we have hypotheses about which of the motivation scores should be most strongly associated with perfectionism and would like to investigate whether these are accurate. Specifically, prior research suggests that approach goals (be they mastery or performance) should be more strongly associated with self-oriented perfectionism than should avoidance goals.

First, we will conduct a standard multiple regression analysis in order to ascertain the relationships between the goal orientation and perfectionism variables. The regression coefficients, standardized beta weights, and associated statistics appear in Table 6. Based on these results, we conclude that higher scores on mastery approach and performance approach had statistically significantly positive relationships with self-oriented perfectionism scores. Neither of the avoidance goal scores were significantly associated with perfectionism. Together, the goal orientation variables accounted for approximately 16% of the variance in self-oriented perfectionism scores.

Table 6
Regression coefficients, standard errors, test statistic, and p-value for goal orientation and perfectionism regression model

Variable	Coefficient	Beta	Standard error	t	p
Intercept	28.42		5.37	5.29	<0.001
Mastery approach	1.17	0.21	0.34	2.83	0.001
Mastery avoidance	0.47	0.10	0.28	1.69	0.09
Performance approach	0.82	0.22	0.34	2.41	0.02
Performance avoidance	0.21	0.06	0.35	0.60	0.55

Note: $R^2_{Adjusted} = 0.16$

As with ANOVA and the t-test, we need to assess the assumptions underlying multiple regression, normality and homogeneity of variance for the residuals. The QQ-plot of the residuals is interpreted in the same way that we did for the t-test. The closer the observed data coheres to the line, the closer to being normally distributed are the residuals. For this example, the residuals follow the line very closely for the large bulk of the residuals, leading us to conclude that the normality assumption has been satisfied. The homogeneity of variance assumption can be assessed using the fitted by residual and scale-location plots. If homogeneity holds, the plot should be a formless cloud with no evident patterns and the line should be essentially horizontal. Generally speaking, this appears to be the case in the plots, leading to the conclusion of variance homogeneity for the residuals. Finally, the residuals versus leverage plot identifies individual data points that are highly influential in the solution. We can see that there is one individual who had a high leverage value, indicating that they had unusual scores on the independent variables. Given that it is a single individual, we do not need to be overly concerned with this issue.

Now that we have fit the basic regression model and assessed the assumptions associated with it, we can turn our attention to the comparison of the relative importance of the independent variables with respect to their relationships to self-oriented perfectionism. As was noted above, research has revealed that the beta weight for a given independent variable is not useful for determining variable importance because they do not account for the relationships among the independent variables themselves (Pedhazur, 1997; Capraro & Capraro, 2001). Therefore, we will not make such comparisons for this example.

As we discussed above, a better approach for assessing the relative importance of independent variables in the model is DA. Our goal is to understand whether the approach variables are relatively more important predictors of self-oriented perfectionism than are the avoidance predictors. The general dominance statistic values for each variable appear in Table 7. Mastery approach had the largest general dominance value, followed by performance approach, mastery avoidance, and performance avoidance. The bootstrap analysis shows that mastery approach yielded the largest dominance statistic vis-à-vis each of the other independent variables. Performance approach was the second most dominant predictor, dominating performance approach in 68% of the bootstrap samples and dominating performance avoidance in 90% of the bootstrap samples. Mastery avoidance dominated performance avoidance in a majority of bootstrap samples (0.58), and performance avoidance was not dominant for a majority of bootstrap samples versus any of the other predictors.

Table 7
General dominance values and proportion of bootstrap samples for which row variable dominates column variable for goal orientation variables with respect to self-oriented perfectionism

Variable	Bootstrap DA results				
	General dominance	Mastery approach	Mastery avoidance	Performance approach	Performance avoidance
Mastery approach	0.049		0.73	0.59	0.77
Mastery avoidance	0.038	0.27		0.32	0.58
Performance approach	0.047	0.41		0.68	0.90
Performance avoidance	0.033	0.23	0.42	0.10	

We can now summarize the set of regression results in order to obtain a complete picture of the relationships between self-oriented perfectionism and the motivation variables. The regression model results revealed that higher scores on either of the approach goal orientation variables were associated with higher scores on self-oriented perfectionism. In both cases, there was an approximately 20% (0.2) standard deviation increase in perfectionism for a one-point increase in the approach variables. On the other hand, neither of the avoidance goal orientation scores were found to be associated with self-oriented perfectionism. Together, the goal orientation variables were associated with approximately 16% of the variability in perfectionism scores.

With respect to the relative importance of the achievement goal variables, DA revealed that mastery approach might be slightly more strongly related to perfectionism than performance approach, based on the bootstrap results. In 59% of the replications, mastery approach had a larger dominance coefficient than performance approach. At the same time, the mastery approach general dominance statistic was slightly larger than that for performance approach (0.049 vs 0.047), though the values were quite similar . The Bayes factor analysis provided additional evidence that the approach goal orientation variables were of roughly equal importance with respect to perfectionism, and that both were more important in this regard than the avoidance goal orientation variables. Thus, considering the totality of evidence, we would conclude that higher mastery and performance approach goal orientations are associated with greater levels of perfectionism but that it is not possible to discern a difference in their importance from one another.

Discussion

Much research in education, psychology, and social work involves analyzing data using tried and true statistical techniques such as the t-test, ANOVA, and linear regression. These methods allow researchers to ascertain whether one or more independent variables are related to a dependent variable, whether in the form of group differences or linear relationships, through the use of hypothesis testing. However, it is also the case that sole reliance on the standard null hypothesis testing approach to research has been called into question as being too limited in terms of what it reveals (Colling & Szucs, 2021). In addition, the replication crisis in social sciences may be due in part to an overreliance on simple hypothesis tests. Therefore, it has been recommended that researchers include additional information about the relationships of interest (Haig, 2017). In response to this call for a more holistic approach to understanding relationships in the data, this manuscript described statistical techniques that can be incorporated with the standard null hypothesis testing approach.

The combined approach to addressing research questions involving univariate group comparisons and assessment of relationships between variables involves the use of effect sizes and the Bayes Factor, as well as confidence intervals when appropriate. This combination of statistical techniques yields to the researcher information not only about statistical significance, but also about the relative magnitude of the effects present in the data and about the likelihood of various potential hypotheses being true in the population. Thus, the researcher can not only make statements regarding the likelihood of group differences or relationships between variables in the population, but can also describe the relative probability of various possible hypotheses and about the magnitudes of the effects that we see in the population. Together, these characterizations should provide the researcher with a greater sense of the full nature of the variable relationships in their data, and in the population more broadly.

Table 8
Bayes factors and posterior probabilities for hypotheses regarding self-oriented perfectionism regression

Hypothesis	Bayes factor*	Probability
MAP = MAV = PAP = PAV	0	0
MAP = MAV & PAP = PAV	36.88	0.13
MAP = PAP > MAV = PAV	164.48	0.56
MAP = PAP & MAV = PAV	89.31	0.30
MAP > PAP > MAV > PAV	4.36	0.01

Note: *Likelihood of hypothesis compared to unconstrained hypothesis

Figure 2
Diagnostic plots for regression model

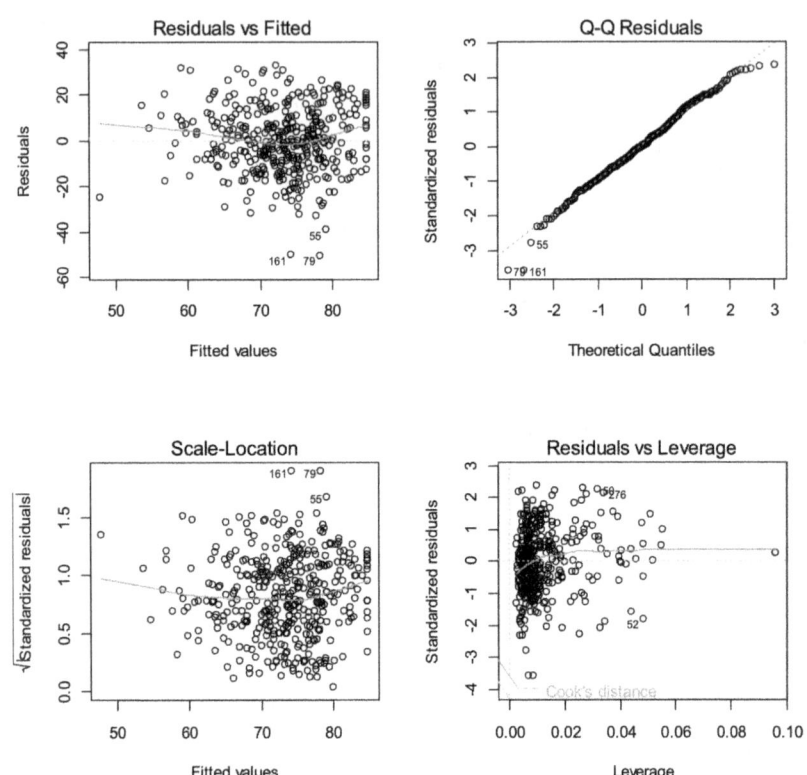

References

Azen, R. & Budescu, D.V. (2003). The dominance analysis approach for comparing predictors in multiple regression. *Psychological Methods, 8,* 129-148. https://doi.org/10.1037/1082-989X.8.2.129

Azen, R. & Traxel, N. (2009). Using dominance analysis to determine predictor importance in logistic regression. *Journal of Educational and Behavioral Statistics, 34,* 319-347. https://www.jstor.org/stable/40263507

Braun, M.T., Converse, P.D., & Oswald, F.L. (2019). The accuracy of dominance analysis as a metric to assess relative importance: The joint impact of sampling error variance and measurement unreliability. *The Journal of Applied Psychology, 104,* 593-602. https://doi.org/10.1037/apl0000361

Capraro, M. M., Capraro, R. M., & Henson, R. K. (2001). Measurement error of scores on the Mathematics Anxiety Rating Scale across studies. *Educational and Psychological Measurement, 61(3),* 373–386. https://doi.org/10.1177/00131640121971266

Cohen, J. (1988). *Statistical power analysis for the behavioral sciences*. L. Erlbaum Associates.
Colling, L.J. & Szucs, D. (2021). Statistical inference and the replication crisis. *Review of Philosophy and Psychology, 12*, 121-147. https://doi.org/10.1007/s13164-018-0421-4
Djonko-Moore, C.M. (2022). Diversity education and early childhood teachers' motivation to remain in teaching: An exploration. *Journal of Early Childhood Teacher Education, 43*(1), 35-53. https://doi:10.1080/10901027.2020.1806151
Field, A. (2013). *Discovering statistics using IBM SPSS Statistics*. Sage.
Gliner, J.A., Leech, N.L., & Morgan, G.A. (2002). Problems with null hypothesis significance testing (NHST): What do the textbooks say? *The Journal of Experimental Education, 71*(1), 83-92. https://doi.org/10.1080/00220970209602058
Gu, X. (2022). Assessing the relative importance of predictors in latent regression models. *Structural Equation Modeling: A Multidisciplinary Journal, 29*(4), 569-583. https://doi.org/10.1080/10705511.2021.2025377
Gu, X., Hoijtink, H., Mulder, J., & van Lissa, C. (2021). bain: Bayes factors for informative hypotheses. (Version 0.2.8) [R package].
Gu, X., Mulder, J., & Hoijtink, H. (2018). Approximated adjusted fractional Bayes factors: A general method for testing informative hypotheses. *British Journal of Mathematical and Statistical Psychology, 71*(2), 229-261. https://doi.org/10.1111/bmsp.12110
Haig, B.D. (2017). Tests of statistical significance made sound. *Educational and Psychological Measurement, 77*(3), 489-506. https://doi.org/10.1177/0013164416667981
Kang, G. (2021). Developmental trends in early childhood and their predictors from an Indian birth cohort. *BMC Public Health, 21*, 1-8. https://doi.org/10.1186/s12889-021-11147-3
Kaplan, D. (2014). Bayesian Statistics for the Social Sciences. New York: Guilford Press.
Koshy, B., Srinivasan, M., Bose, A., John, S., Mohan, V.R., Roshan, R., Ramanujam, K., &
Kroes, A.D.A. & Finley, J.R. (2023). Demystifying omega squared: Practical guidance for effect size in common analysis of variance designs. *Psychological Methods*, Advance online publication. https://doi.org/10.1037/met0000581
Lichand, G., Neto, O.L., & Phuka, J.C. (2022). The early childhood development replication crisis, and how wearable technologies could help overcome it. *SSRN Electronic Journal, 4*, 1-20. http://dx.doi.org/10.2139/ssrn.4162049 Pedhazur, E.J. (1997) *Multiple Regression in Behavioral Research: An Explanation and Prediction*. Holt, Rinehart & Winston, New York.
R Core Team. (2023). *R: A language and environment for statistical computing*. R Foundation for Statistical Computing. https://www.R-project.org/.
Schachter, R.E., Spear, C.F., Piasta, S.B., Justice, L.M., & Logan, J.A.R. (2016). Early childhood educators' knowledge, beliefs, education, experiences, and children's language- and literacy-learning opportunities: What is the connection? *Early Childhood Research Quarterly, 36*(3), 281-294. https://doi:10.1016/J.ECRESQ.2016.01.008

Slavin, R. & Smith, D. (2009). The relationship between sample sizes and effect sizes in systematic reviews in education. *Educational Evaluation and Policy Analysis, 31*(4), 500-506. https://doi.org/10.3102/0162373709352369

Tonidandel, S., LeBreton, J.M., & Johnson, J. (2009). Determining the statistical significance of relative weights. *Psychological Methods, 14,* 387-399. https://doi.org/10.1037/a0017735

Wilcox, R.R. & Serang, S. (2017). Hypothesis testing, p-values, confidence intervals, measures of effect size, and Bayesian methods in light of modern robust techniques. *Educational and Psychological Measurement, 77*(4), 673-689. doi: 10.1177/0013164416667983

Wright, D.B. (2006). Comparing groups in a before-after design: When t-test and ANCOVA produce different results. *British Journal of Educational Psychology, 76*(3), 663-675. https://doi.org/10.1348/000709905X52210

Using Multilevel Modeling to Understand Nested Data

W. Holmes Finch

Abstract

Researchers in the social sciences often work with nested data, in which individuals are collected in higher level clusters. For example, educational research often involves working with samples in which students are nested within schools. Standard data analyses, such as regression and analysis of variance (ANOVA), yield statistically biased results when this nested structure is ignored. One widely used and effective approach for handling such nested data is multilevel modeling. The purpose of this manuscript is to review the basics of multilevel modeling and to provide the reader with a fully worked example in which the analytic approach and results are described in full. The online supplemental materials that go with this paper also provide the reader with the computational resources necessary to conduct these analyses.

Perhaps the most widely used statistical techniques in the social sciences are based on the linear model that underlies such common statistical methods as regression and analysis of variance (ANOVA). This model rests on several assumptions regarding the nature of the data in the population, including normality, variance homogeneity, and independence of the residuals. This latter assumption essentially means that there are no relationships among individuals in the sample for the dependent variable, once the independent variables in the analysis are accounted for. In other words, there is nothing linking scores on the dependent variable values other than the independent variables included in the linear model. In many real world situations, however, this assumption is very likely to be violated.

For example, a researcher interested in the impact of a new teaching method on achievement test scores for first graders might randomly select schools for placement in either a treatment or control group, meaning that all students in the school are study participants. It would be reasonable to assume that the school itself, above and beyond the treatment condition, would have an impact on test performance of the students, due to the teachers, curriculum used in the instruction, quality of the facilities, etc. This school-based impact would manifest itself as a correlation in achievement test scores among individuals attending that school. Thus, if we were to use a simple one-way ANOVA to compare the achievement test means for the treatment and control groups with such cluster sampled data, we would likely be violating the assumption of independent errors because a factor beyond treatment condition (in this case the school) would have an additional impact on the outcome variable. We typically refer to the data structure described above as nested, meaning that individual data points at one level (e.g. student) appear in only one level of a higher-level variable such as school. In our example, students are nested within school leading to the possibility that schools may impact relationships among student scores on the achievement test.

The focus of this article is on using a multilevel model (MLM) to deal with data collected from nested designs. These MLMs account for the correlations among individuals nested within the same clustering variable (e.g., students nested within schools). When standard statistical models such as regression are used with nested data, the results will be statistically biased because they do not account for the impact of nesting. Multilevel models, on the other hand, include the effects of nesting in the estimation of model parameters such as regression coefficients. The manuscript is organized as follows. First, we discuss problems associated with ignoring nesting in our data, followed by a brief review of the intraclass correlation, which is a key statistic in understanding the degree to which nesting impacts the analysis. Next, we will review two very common multilevel modeling frameworks, the random intercept and random slopes models. Finally, we will work through an extended example demonstrating the use of the multilevel model in practice.

Pitfalls of Ignoring Multilevel Data Structure

When researchers apply standard statistical methods to multilevel data, such as the regression model, the assumption of independent errors is violated. For example, if we have achievement test scores from a sample of students who attend several different schools, it would be reasonable to believe that those attending the same school will have scores that are more highly correlated with one another than they are with scores from students attending other schools. This within-school correlation would be due, for example, to having a common set of teachers, a common teaching curriculum, coming from a common community, or a single set of administrative policies, among numerous other reasons. The within-school correlation will in turn result in an inappropriate estimate of the of the standard errors for the model parameters, which in turn will lead to errors of statistical inference, such as *p*-values smaller than they really should be and the resulting rejection of null effects above the stated Type I error rate, regarding the parameters.

In addition to the underestimation of the standard error, another problem with ignoring the multilevel structure of data is that we may miss important relationships involving each level in the data. Recall that in our example, there are two levels of sampling: students (level 1) are nested in schools (level 2). By ignoring information about the school, for example, we may well miss important variables at the school level that help to explain performance at the examinee level. Therefore, beyond the known problem with misestimating standard errors, we also estimate an incorrect model for understanding the outcome variable of interest. In the context of multilevel models, inclusion of variables at each level is relatively simple, as are interactions among variables at different levels. This greater model complexity in turn may lead to greater understanding of the phenomenon under study.

Intraclass Correlation

In cases where individuals are clustered or nested within a higher-level unit (e.g., classrooms, schools, school districts), it is possible to estimate the correlation among individual's scores within the cluster/nested structure using the intraclass correlation (). The ρ_I can also be interpreted as a measure of the proportion of variation in the dependent variable that is due to the clustering variable (e.g., school). It is calculated as

$$\rho_I = \frac{\tau^2}{(\tau^2 + \sigma^2)} \tag{1}$$

where

τ^2 = Population variance between clusters

σ^2 = Population variance within clusters

Higher values of ρ_I indicate that a greater share of the total variation in the outcome measure is associated with cluster membership; i.e. there is a relatively strong relationship among the scores for two individuals from the same cluster. Another way to frame this issue is that individuals within the same cluster (e.g. school) are more alike on the measured variable than they are like those in other clusters. Thus, larger values of the intraclass correlation (ICC) mean that we must be more cognizant of employing multilevel modeling strategies in our data analysis.

Random Intercept Model

Before examining the multilevel model, we should first review the basic simple linear regression model of equation:

$$y = \beta_0 + \beta_1 x + \varepsilon. \tag{2}$$

Here, the dependent variable y is expressed as a function of an independent variable, x, multiplied by a slope coefficient, β_1, an intercept, β_0, and random variation from subject to subject, ε. The intercept is the mean of y when the value of x is 0. In the context of a single level regression model such as this, there is one intercept that is common to all individuals in the population of interest. However, when individuals are clustered together in some fashion (e.g. within schools), there will potentially be a separate intercept for each of these clusters; that is, there may be different means for the dependent variable for x=0 across the different clusters. It should also be noted that in this discussion we are considering only the case where the intercept is cluster specific, but it is also possible for β_1 to vary by group, as we shall see below.

As we continue our discussion of multilevel modeling notation and structure we will begin with the most basic multilevel model, predicting the outcome from just an intercept which we will allow to vary randomly for each group.

$$y_{ij} = \beta_{0j} + \varepsilon_{ij} \qquad (3)$$

where

y_{ij} = Value of the dependent variable for individual i in cluster j

β_{0j} = Intercept for cluster j

ε_{ij} = Random error for individual i in cluster j

Allowing the intercept to differ across clusters, as in equation (3), leads to the random intercept which in turn is expressed as

$$\beta_{0j} = \gamma_{00} + U_{0jj} \qquad (4)$$

where

γ_{00} = Average or general intercept value that holds across clusters

U_{0j} = Cluster specific effect on the intercept

We can think of γ_{00} as a fixed effect because it remains constant across all clusters, and U_{0j} is a random effect because it varies from cluster to cluster. Therefore, for a MLM we are interested not only in some general mean value for y when x is 0 for all individuals in the population (y_{00}), but also the deviation between the overall mean and the cluster specific effects for the intercept (U_{0j}). If we go on to assume that the clusters are a random sample from the population of all such clusters, then we can treat U_{0j} as a kind of residual effect on y_{ij}, very similar to how we think of ε. In that case, U_{0j} is assumed to be drawn randomly from a population with a mean of 0 (recall U_{0j} is a deviation from the fixed effect) and a variance, τ^2. Furthermore, we assume that τ^2 and σ^2, the variance of e, are uncorrelated. We have already discussed τ^2 and its role in calculating , which is an estimate of in equation (1). In addition, τ^2 can also be viewed as the impact of the cluster on the dependent variable, and therefore testing it for statistical significance is equivalent to testing the null hypothesis that cluster (e.g. school) has no impact on the dependent variable. If we substitute the two components of the random intercept into model (2), we get

$$y = \gamma_{00} + U_{0j} + \beta_1 x + \varepsilon \tag{5}$$

This represents the full random intercept model.

Often in MLM, we begin our analysis of a dataset with this simple random intercept model, known as the null model, which takes the form

$$y_{ij} = \gamma_{00} + U_{0j} + \varepsilon_{ij} \tag{6}$$

While the null model does not provide information regarding the impact of specific independent variables on the dependent variable, it does yield important information regarding how variation in y is partitioned between variance due to the individuals within clusters σ^2 and the variance between the clusters τ^2. The total variance of y is simply the sum of σ^2 and τ^2. In addition, as we have already seen, these values can be used to estimate ρ_I.

Random Slopes Model

We can express the random intercept model in equation (5) as having two levels, one for individuals and another for clusters.

As an example, if we have a single independent variable (x_{ij}) at the individual level (level-1) to the model, we have

$$y_{ij} = \gamma_{00} + \gamma_{10} x_{ij} + U_{0j} + \varepsilon_{ij} \tag{7}$$

This model can then be expressed in two separate levels as:

Level 1: $y_{ij} = \beta_0 + \beta_{1j} + \varepsilon_{ij}$ \hfill (8)

Level 2: $\beta_{0j} = \gamma_{00} + U_{0j}$ \hfill (9)

$\beta_{1j} = \gamma_{10}$ \hfill (10)

This model now includes the predictor and the slope relating it to the dependent variable, γ_{10}, which we acknowledge as being at level-1 by the subscript 10. We interpret γ_{10} in the same way that we did β_1 in the linear regression model; i.e. a measure of the impact on y of a 1 unit change in x. In addition, we can estimate ρ_I exactly as before, though now it reflects the correlation between individuals from the same cluster after controlling for the independent variable, x. In this model, both γ_{10} and γ_{00} are fixed effects, while σ^2 and τ^2 remain random.

One implication of the model in equation (7) is that the dependent variable is impacted by variation among individuals (σ^2), variation among clusters (τ^2), an overall mean common to all clusters (γ_{00}), and the independent variable as measured by γ_{10}, which is also common to all clusters. In practice there is no reason that the impact of x on y would need to be common for all clusters, however. In other words, it is entirely possible that rather than having a single γ_{10} common to all clusters, there is actually a unique effect for the cluster of $\gamma_{10} + U1_j$, where γ_{10} is the average relationship of x with y across clusters, and $U1_j$ is the cluster specific variation of the relationship between the two variables. This cluster specific effect is assumed to have a mean of 0 and to vary randomly around γ_{10}. This random slopes model can then be expressed as

$$y_{ij} = \gamma_{00} + \gamma_{10} x_{ij} + U_{0j} + U_{1j} x_{ij} + \varepsilon_{ij} \tag{11}$$

Written in this way, we have separated the model into its fixed

($\gamma_{00} + \gamma_{10}x_{ij}$) and random ($U_{0j} + U_{1j}x_{ij} + \varepsilon_{ij}$) components. Model (11) indicates that there is an interaction between cluster membership (e.g., the school a student attends) and the independent variable, such that the relationship of *x* and *y* is not constant across clusters. We will consider this model, along with the random intercept model in the example below.

Centering

Centering simply refers to the practice of subtracting the mean of a variable from each individual value. This implies that the mean for the sample of the centered variables is 0, and that each individual's (centered) score represents a deviation from the mean, rather than whatever meaning its raw value might have. Centering is a way to deal with large correlations (collinearity) among independent variables in regression (e.g., Iversen, 1991). Likewise, centering is also a useful tool for avoiding collinearity caused by highly correlated random intercepts and slopes in multilevel models (Wooldridge, 2004). Centering also provides a potential advantage when interpreting results. Remember that the intercept is the value of the dependent variable when the independent variable is set equal to 0. In many applications the independent variable cannot reasonably be 0 (e.g., a measure of vocabulary), however, which essentially renders the intercept as a necessary value for fitting the regression line but not one that has a readily interpretable value. However, when *x* has been centered, the intercept represents the value of the dependent variable when the independent is at its mean. This is a much more useful interpretation for researchers in many situations, and yet another reason why centering is an important aspect of modeling, particularly in the multilevel context.

Probably the most common approach to centering is to calculate the difference between each individual's score and the overall or grand mean across the entire sample. This grand mean centering is the most commonly used in practice (Bickel, 2007). An alternative approach, known as group mean centering, is to calculate the difference between each individual score and the mean of the cluster to which they belong. In our school example, grand mean centering would involve calculating the difference between each score and the overall mean across schools, while group mean centering would lead the researcher to calculate the difference between each score and the mean for their school. While there is some disagreement in the literature regarding which approach might be best at reducing the harmful effects of collinearity (Snijders & Bosker, 1999), researchers have demonstrated that in most cases either will work well in this regard (Kreft et al., 1995). Therefore, the choice of which approach to use must be made on substantive grounds regarding the nature of the relationship between x and y. By using grand mean centering, we are implicitly comparing individuals to one another (in the form of the overall mean) across the entire sample. On the other hand, when using group mean centering we are placing each individual in relative position on x within their cluster. Thus, in our school example, using the group mean centered values of vocabulary in the analysis would mean that we are investigating the relationship between a student's relative vocabulary score in their school and their reading score. In contrast, the use of grand mean centering would examine the relationship between a student's relative standing in the sample as a whole on vocabulary and the reading score. This latter interpretation would be equivalent conceptually to using the raw score, while the group mean centering would not. The choice of which type of centering, or whether to use centering at all, is dependent on what the researcher is most interested in studying.

Comparing Model Fit

Often, one wishes to compare the fit of multiple models in order to identify a best-fitting model given the data. There are two different types of model fit information: information indices such as the Akaike information criterion (AIC) and the Bayesian information criterion (BIC), and the chi square test of model fit. AIC and BIC reflect how well the model predicts values of the dependent variable (i.e., how well the model fits the data) with a penalty added for more complexity. In general, models with more independent variables fit the data better, regardless of the true relationships between these variables and the outcome. Therefore, it is important to penalize more complex models to ensure that including more independent variables does in fact yield better predictions of the dependent variable. Models with smaller values of the AIC and BIC are said to fit the data better.

When we are working with nested models, where one model is a more constrained (i.e. simpler) version of another, we may wish to test whether overall fit of the two models differs significantly (as opposed to using AIC and BIC statistics which are more general model comparison statistics and can't provide this level of detail). Such hypothesis testing is possible using the chi-square difference test based on the deviance statistic, also referred to as the likelihood ratio test. When the fits of nested models are being compared, the difference in chi-square values for each model deviance can be used to compare model fit. The null hypothesis of the likelihood ratio test is that the models fit the data equally well. Therefore, if the difference test is not statistically significant, we would conclude that the simpler model is preferable because it yields equivalent fit to the more complex model. On the other hand, a rejection of the null hypothesis would lead the researcher to retain the more complex model.

MLM Example

In order to demonstrate the use of MLM, we will examine data from the Program in International Literacy Study (PIRLS; National Center for Educational Statistics, 2021). This study involves the assessment of reading achievement for elementary school students from multiple nations. In addition to the reading assessment, data on student attitudes towards reading, early literacy activities, and family socioeconomic status (SES) are collected as part of the PIRLS program. For the purposes of this demonstration, the outcome variable was the reading assessment score, with level-1 being students and level-2 being schools. A score reflecting early literacy activities was used as a level-1 independent variable and the mean family SES for each school was the level-2 independent variable. A null model with no predictor variables was fit to the data in order to obtain the ICC. In addition, a random intercepts model including early literacy activities, a random intercepts and slopes model including early literacy activities, and a random intercepts model including early literacy activities and school mean SES as independent variables will be fit to the data as well. All analyses were conducted using SPSS. A brief tutorial demonstrating these analyses is available at https://holmesfinch.substack.com/.

Null Model

The first step in exploring multilevel data structures is to fit a null model, which includes only the intercept and no independent variables. The purpose for fitting this model is to obtain estimates for the level-2 variance (intercept variance) and the variability associated with individuals (residual variance). These values are used to calculate the ICC (see equation 1) thereby giving us insights into the degree to which schools alone contribute to the reading scores. For this example, the intercept variance reflects differences in mean reading achievement scores across schools, and the residual variance reflects variability in reading scores for students within the same schools.

When only the random intercept term was included in the model, the residual (student specific) variance was 9968.27 and the intercept (school mean reading difference) variance was 3331.53, as seen in Table 1. These values are in and of themselves not particularly informative. However, they can be used to calculate the ICC, which appears in the last column in Table 1. The ICC value of 0.25 can be interpreted as the proportion of variability in the reading scores associated with the school that students attend; i.e., 25%. Alternatively, the ICC reflects the correlation between reading scores for students within the same school. In other words, the correlation between reading scores is 0.25. This value is sufficiently high for us to remain in the multilevel modeling framework. In other words, the correlations among the individuals within the same schools is high enough that we cannot assume that their residuals are uncorrelated, thereby violating a major assumption underlying standard regression models. Finally, the intercept estimate for the null model, which is the mean reading test score across schools, was 489.20, with a 95% confidence interval of 485.31 to 493.10. Thus, there is a 0.95 probability that the true mean reading test score is between these two values.

Table 1
Random variance values for each multilevel model

Model	Residual variance	Intercept variance	Slope variance	ICC	R^2
Null	9968.27	3331.53*	NA	0.25	0
Random intercept	9230.11	2529.25*	NA	0.22	0.07
Cross levels	9236.15	1374.33*	NA	0.13	0.10
Random slope	9172.27	1688.95*	8.04*	0.16	0.09

Note: *$p < 0.05$

Random Intercept Model

Having established the need for a multilevel model based on the ICC value, we can use it to examine the relationship between the reading achievement score and a measure of early literacy activities. We'll start with a random intercept model, which allows for different mean reading scores across the schools, as described above. The fit statistics for the null and random intercept models appear in Table 2. Each of the relative fit statistics had a lower value for the random intercept model, as compared to the null model, indicating that it provides a better fit; i.e., is more supported statistically. In addition, the likelihood ratio test comparing the fit of the two models was statistically significant, providing further support for the conclusion that the random intercept provides better fit to the data.

The ICC for the random intercept model was 0.22 (Table 1) reflects the proportion of variance in reading test scores associated with schools, after accounting for preliteracy activities. The R^2 value for the fixed effects of the model is 0.07, meaning that 7% of the variability in reading scores is accounted for by early literacy activities. We can see that this value was 0.03 less than when there were no fixed effects in the model; i.e., including preliteracy activity score reduces the impact of schools by 0.03. It should be noted that there is no one best estimate of R^2 in the context of MLMs (Nakagawa & Schielzeth, 2013). We have used the approach outlined by Rights & Sterba (2019) in this example. The coefficient for early literacy activities and the intercept appears in Table 3. The coefficient was 13.77, meaning that children who engaged in more early literacy activities had higher reading test scores in second grade. In linear models (including multilevel models such as the ones we are discussing), the intercept reflects the value of the dependent variable when the independent variable has a value of 0. For this study, a 0 score for early literacy means that the child did not engage in any early literacy activities prior to entering school. Thus, when children did not have any early literacy activities, the mean reading test score is predicted to be 344.54. Finally, it should be noted that in some cases (though not this one), 0 is not a reasonable value for the independent variable, in which case we would need to interpret the intercept with care.

Table 2
Model fit statistics

Model	AIC	BIC
Null	1844230.31	1844250.18
Random intercept	1486864.12	1486883.58
Cross levels	1485548.99	1485568.45
Random slope	1485293.31	1485328.50

Table 3
Fixed effects coefficients

Variable	Coefficient	Standard error	p	CI lower bound	CI upper bound
Null model					
Intercept	489.20	1.98	< 0.001	485.31	493.10
Random intercept model					
Intercept	344.54	2.28	< 0.001	340.06	349.01
Early literacy	13.77	0.13	< 0.001	13.51	14.04
Cross levels model					
Intercept	151.84	8.71	< 0.001	134.74	168.94
Early literacy	13.61	0.14	< 0.001	13.34	13.87
School SES	21.13	0.94	< 0.001	19.29	22.96
Random slope					
Intercept	173.42	10.55	< 0.001	152.70	191.13
Early literacy	13.47	0.20	< 0.001	13.08	13.86
School SES	18.92	1.13	< 0.001	16.70	21.13

Cross Levels Interaction Model

Next, we will include a school level independent variable, the average family SES, along with early literacy activities at the child level. The relative fit statistics (Table 2) suggest that this cross levels model provides better fit to the data than the model with early literacy alone (random intercept model). In addition, the likelihood ratio test comparing the two models was statistically significant, indicating that inclusion of the school mean family SES improved the model fit.

The ICC for the cross levels model fell to 0.13 from 0.22 for the random intercept model (Table 1). In other words, the variation in reading test scores accounted for by schools after the effect of mean family SES was removed declined from 0.22 to 0.13. In addition, the fixed effects (early literacy activities and school mean family SES) accounted for 10% of the variance in reading test scores. The coefficients for early literacy and the school mean family SES appear in Table 3. The coefficient for early literacy in this model is quite similar to that for the random intercept model, again showing that greater early literacy activities were associated with higher reading test scores. The mean family SES coefficient was also positive, indicating that children attending schools with higher mean family SES had higher reading achievement test scores.

Random Slopes Model

Finally, we will examine a random slopes model, which allows the relationship between early literacy activities and reading test scores to differ from one school to another. This model includes fixed effects for early literacy activities, school mean family SES, the random intercept for early literacy activities, and the random intercept for early literacy activities. The relative fit statistics for this model (Table 2) were lower than for the cross levels model, as well as for the others included in this demonstration. In addition, the likelihood ratio comparing the random slopes model with the cross levels model was statistically significant. Taken together, these results reveal that the random slopes model provided better fit to the data than did the cross levels.

The ICC for the random slopes model was 0.16, meaning that after accounting for the early literacy and school mean family SES, as well as the random intercept and random slope components, schools accounted for approximately 16% of the variance in the reading test scores. The fixed effects accounted for approximately 9% of the variability in reading test scores. In addition, both the intercept and slope variances were statistically significant, meaning that mean reading scores differed across schools, as did the relationship between early literacy activities and reading achievement. The fixed effects coefficients for early literacy and school SES appear in Table 3. As with the cross levels model, the coefficients for early literacy and school SES were statistically significant and positive, meaning that children who engaged in more early literacy activities and those who attended schools with higher mean family SES generally performed better on the reading assessment.

Summary of Results

Considering the modeling results together, we would conclude that the statistically optimal model includes early literacy activities and school mean family SES as fixed effects predictors, and allows random effects for both the intercept and slope. Thus, students who attended schools with higher mean SES and who engaged in more early literacy activities generally performed better on the reading assessment. In addition, mean reading test scores differed across the schools. Finally, the relationship of early literacy activities and reading was not the same across schools. In some schools engaging in more early literacy activities was more strongly related to reading test performance than was the case in other schools.

Discussion

Multilevel data structure is very common in educational and psychological research. Students may be nested within classrooms and/or schools, patients may be nested within clinics, and children may be nested within friend groups, for example. As we have seen, ignoring this structure can result in biased estimates of regression coefficients and their standard errors. Such bias in turn can yield incorrect statistical results, leading the researcher to erroneous conclusions regarding their research questions and hypotheses. Fortunately, there are a set of well understood modeling approaches to handle such situations, in the form of multilevel models. We have examined how a number of such approaches can be applied to a very typical research scenario involving prediction of a continuous dependent variable with multiple independent variables for children who are nested in schools. We fit a series of statistical models sequentially and then compared their fit in order to determine which yielded the optimal statistical results. For this example, we saw that this optimal model included independent variables at both the student and school levels, and allowed for different school mean reading scores and different relationships between the student level predictor and the outcome. Of course, in other research scenarios this model may not always yield the best fit to the data.

We should conclude here by briefly mentioning extensions of the multilevel modeling framework that might prove useful to researchers. First, it is possible to have more than two levels. For example, the analyses described above included data only from the United States. However, the larger dataset includes several nations. Thus, if we were to replicate these analyses for the full set of data, we would use a three-level model where students are nested within school, which are in turn nested within nation. The same statistics and modeling strategy that we used for this example would be applied in the three (or even four) level case. Second, the multilevel modeling paradigm can be applied to situations in which the dependent variable is categorical, involves counts, or reflects time until an event of interest occurs. Multilevel modeling can also be applied when there are multiple dependent variables, as in multilevel multivariate analysis of variance. Finally, there have been recent advancements for applying the multilevel framework to latent variable models such as factor analysis, structural equation models, and latent class analysis. In short, multilevel modeling can now be applied to virtually any research scenario where data are collected in a multilevel way.

With respect to software, researchers have several options. Most of the analyses demonstrated here were done using SPSS, with a little assistance from R. A primary advantage of SPSS is its easy-to-use interface. The R software environment, while more difficult to use, does accommodate perhaps the widest array of modeling possibilities. For researchers working in the latent variable framework, the Mplus software package is an excellent choice, as it provides the widest set of options for latent class and various factor models. And finally, both SAS and STATA are also excellent software options, though as with R and Mplus they require some statistical programming. I would conclude by saying that if the researcher is primarily interested in fitting observed variable regression models in the multilevel framework, SPSS provides an easy-to-use option. For those working with more complex or latent variable models, other software packages may be preferable.

Impact statement

This manuscript describes a statistical approach to working with multilevel, or nested data. This type of data structure is quite common in educational research and thus should be very useful to researchers in early childhood, who often work with longitudinal data in which change is common and of interest.

References

Bickel, R. (2007). *Multilevel analysis for applied research: It's just regression!* Guilford Press. https://doi.org/10.1111/j.1465-3362.2008.00013_5.x

Iversen, G. (1991). *Contextual analysis*. Sage.

Kreft, I. G. G., de Leeuw, J., & Aiken, L. (1995). The effect of different forms of centering in hierarchical linear models. *Multivariate Behavioral Research, 30*, 1–22. https://doi.org/10.1207/s15327906mbr3001_1

Nakagawa, S. & Schielzeth, H. (2013). A general and simple method for obtaining from generalized linear mixed-effects models. *Methods in Ecology and Evolution, 4(2)*, 133–142. https://doi.org/10.1111/J2041-210x.2012.00261.X

National Center for Educational Statistics. (2021). Progress in International Reading Literacy Study (PIRLS). https://nces.ed.gov/surveys/pirls/pirls2021/index.asp.

Rights, J. D., & Sterba, S. K. (2019). Quantifying explained variance in multilevel models: An integrative framework for defining R-squared measures. *Psychological Methods, 24(3)*, 309–338. https://doi.org/10.1037/met0000184

Snijders, T., & Bosker, R. (1999). *Multilevel analysis: An introduction to basic and advanced multilevel modeling*. Sage.

Wooldridge, J. (2004). *Fixed effects and related estimators for correlated random coefficient and treatment effect panel data models*. Department of Economics, Michigan State University.

A Tutorial for Identifying and Comparing Changepoints in Developmental Trajectories

W. Holmes Finch

Abstract

Researchers in a variety of social science fields work with sequential data, such as measurements made over time. In some instances, one or more of the moments (e.g., mean, variance) of the series may change abruptly at some point in the sequence, yielding what is known as a changepoint. There is a broad literature describing methods for changepoint detection. Researchers working with multiple sequential series containing changepoints may be interested in comparing the locations of these changes. This manuscript demonstrates how a researcher can detect changepoints and compare them between two or more time series.

Of primary interest to researchers working with young children is the study of development and change. Given the often-rapid transitions that humans make early in life, researchers need to collect sequential, or time series data and need the tools to analyze these data once collected. In addition, for some research scenarios it may be important to detect points within the data sequence where the measured process changes. For example, educational researchers investigating language development may be interested in determining when major shifts in speech occur. Similarly, a psychologist may be interested in detecting changepoints in a child's reading achievement over the course of multiple years. Researchers in other fields, including physical education (Carlson et al., 2008), family studies (Chen & Escarce, 2010), educational technology (Espinosa et al., 2006), and emotional and moral development (Hoemann et al., 2019) may also encounter situations in which they need to identify changepoints with respect to the mean, variance, or both aspects of a time series process. In this context, a time series process is a scenario in which the value of a variable at one time (t) is related to the value of the variable at one or more previous time points.

In addition to detecting the location of such changepoints, there may also be situations in which researchers need to compare changepoint locations for two or more independent series containing measures of the same entity. For example, behavior analysts working with individual children frequently employ an approach involving the administration of a specific intervention, after a period of baseline data collection in which behavior frequency is measured on a daily basis. This intervention might be designed to reduce the prevalence of some problem behavior, and the baseline data collection period is designed to establish the level of the behavior prior to the introduction of the intervention. The behavior analyst would continue to monitor the behavior of the child daily over an extended period of time, in order to determine whether behavior prevalence declined, presumably in response to the intervention. With only one child, standard changepoint detection methods (to be discussed below) might be employed in order to determine where in the time series the prevalence of the behavior changed, if it did. If this intervention strategy were applied to a second child, we would have access to a second time series dataset to which the changepoint analysis could also be applied. The behavior analysis may then be interested in determining whether the changepoints for the two children were at the same locations in the time series. Standard approaches to changepoint detection do not lend themselves to such comparisons, as they do not provide the mechanism for formally testing the null hypothesis that two series have the same changepoint.

The focus of this paper is on demonstrating how researchers can detect changepoints in a set of data and how they can compare the locations of these points for two or more sets of measurements. The computer code used to conduct these analyses, along with example data are available at https://holmesfinch.substack.com/. The paper is organized as follows: First, a brief discussion of changepoint detection methods is provided, followed by a description of the model for comparing changepoint location that is the focus of the current study. Next, a complete example involving the identification and comparison of changepoints is given, followed by a discussion of the utility of changepoint detection and comparison. Finally, we would note that although much technical detail is provided below, the reader who is primarily interested in applying the changepoint detection and comparison methodologies can devote their primary attention to the extended worked example that follows the technical explication.

Change Point Detection

When researchers make sequential measurements of variable for one or more individuals, the resulting time series data is defined as

$$y1:n=(y_1, y_2, \ldots, y_n) \tag{1}$$

In turn, a changepoint is defined as occurring at point y_T if some statistical aspect of the population (e.g., mean, variance) in the measurements for y_1 through y_T are different than those for y_{T+1} through y_n. Although this definition refers to the presence of only a single changepoint, a time series may have multiple changepoints, with the definition being expanded to incorporate the presence of multiple segments within the series, each having a different population mean and/or variance from those of the previous segment. Changepoints are integers between 1 and n-1 thereby creating multiple segments within the time series, and are differentiated by the different population parameter values. Figure 1 displays examples of time series with changepoints for the mean and variance, respectively.

There exist several methods for detecting the number and location of changepoints within a given time series. For a more detailed technical discussion of these approaches, a number of useful sources are available (Aminikhanghahi & Cook, 2017; Eckley et al., 2011; Hukov & Kirch, 2008; Muggeo, 2003; Silva & Teixeira, 2008;). Here we provide a very brief explanation of changepoint detection.

Under the null hypothesis of no changepoint being present in the series, the likelihood function takes the form:

$$ML_0 = \ln(p(y_{1:n}|\theta)) \qquad (2)$$

where

$y_{1:n}$ = Full series from time 1 to n

θ = Parameter estimates based on full series

For the alternative hypothesis that there is a changepoint at T_1, the likelihood function is

$$ML_{T_1} = \ln(p(y_{1:T_1}|\theta_1)) + \ln(p(y_{T_1+1:n}|\theta_2)) \qquad (3)$$

wher

$y_{1:T_1}$ = Series from time 1 to T_1

$y_{T_1+1:n}$ = Series from time $y_{T+1:n}$ to n

θ_1 = Parameter estimates based on segment of series from time 1 to T_1

θ_2 = Parameter estimates based on segment of series from time T_{1+1} to n

Estimates of the parameters are then obtained to minimize the two likelihood functions, which are used in turn to construct a test of the null hypothesis of no changepoints being present in the time series based on the test statistic

$$\lambda = 2(ML_{T_1} - ML_0) \qquad (4)$$

In short, the likelihood of the no changepoint model to fit the observed data (ML_0) is compared with the likelihood of the single changepoint model to fit the data (ML_{T_1}) with change at T_1. If the single changepoint likelihood is larger (i.e., it provides a better fit to the data) then we conclude that there is a changepoint at time T_1.

In order to identify the optimal set of changepoints for a given series, a search algorithm is used in conjunction with the likelihood functions described above. This algorithm has an associated cost function that it seeks to minimize, and which is defined as

$$\sum [C(y_{(T_{i-1}+1):T_i})] + \beta f(m) \qquad (5)$$

where

$[CC(y_{(T_{i-1}+1):T_i})]$ = Cost to the likelihood function for segmenting series at T_1

$\beta f(m)$ = Penalty to guard against over fitting the data

There exist several algorithms that utilize this cost function in searching for the optimal set of changepoints for a given dataset, including binary segmentation (Edwards & Cavalli-Sforza, 1965), segment neighborhood search (Auger & Lawrence, 1989), and pruned exact linear time (Killick et al., 2012). Since these are not the focus of the current paper, we refer the interested reader to the references listed above for further discussions regarding their use.

An alternative to the maximum likelihood approach to changepoint detection is based on the use of a Bayesian estimator. Rigailland colleagues (2012) described a Bayesian approach for detecting multiple changepoints in a time series. This Bayesian model involves the specification of the following components:

1. Prior distribution for the number of segments (K) in the series, $P(K)$
2. The conditional distribution of partition m, given K, $P(m|K)$
3. Distribution of parameters (θ_k) unique to each segment, $P(\theta_k)$
4. Measured data with distribution $(y_t | m, k \in m, \theta_k, t \in k) \sim g(\theta_k)$

Given these defining distributions, the probability distribution for the observed data within segment k can then be expressed as

$$P(y_k | \theta_k) = \prod_{t \in k} g(y_t; \theta_k) \qquad (6)$$

where

$g(y_t; \theta_k)$ = Probability distribution function for .

Given conjugate priors for $\theta_{k'}$ constraints on the distribution of the segmentation process, and the factorability of the function, the Bayesian estimator will provide a posterior distribution for the location of the changepoints in the series. An example of a constraint on the segmentation process is that its prior be the uniform distribution (Cleynen & Robin, 2016).

Comparing ChangepointPoint Locations

Within the Bayesian modeling framework, an approach to comparing the changepoint locations for two or more independent time series has been described (Cleynen & Robin, 2016). This model builds on the work by Rigaill and colleagues (2012) with the Bayesian approach to determining the number of changepoints present in a time series. In this context, it is assumed that there are two or more independent time series measured at the same number of points, with the same length, and the same number of segments. These might be the number of discipline referrals at each of two schools each day over the course of a school year. For a problem involving two time series, this approach models the posterior distribution for the difference between the locations of two changepoints, which Cleynen and Robin refer to as the shift. As an example, consider the case where it is of interest to compare the location of changepoint k for the number of discipline referrals in the two schools. The shift value (difference between the changepoint locations) is expressed as

$$\Delta_k = \tau_{k1} - \tau_{k2} \qquad (7)$$

where

τ_{k1} = Changepoint k for time series 1

τ_{k2} = Changepoint k for time series 2

The posterior distribution for is Δ_k

$$P(\Delta_k = d_k | y_1, y_2, k_1, k_2) = \Sigma_t p_{K_1}(t; y_1; k_1) p_{K_1}(t - d_k; y_2; k_2) \qquad (8)$$

where terms are as defined above.

The credible interval (e.g., 95%) for Δ_k can be used in order to determine whether the changepoints for two series are likely to differ in the population. Credible intervals are very similar to confidence intervals with which the reader might be familiar, and reflect a set of values for the difference that are reasonable in the population. If 0 falls within the credible interval, then we would conclude that it is unlikely for the changepoints to differ from one another in the population, whereas if 0 lies outside of the credibility interval, we would conclude that the changepoint locations do likely differ from one another. The point estimate of the changepoint location can be estimated using the mean or median of the posterior distribution in equation (8). Cleynen and Robin (2016) describe an extension to this Bayesian approach that can be used to ascertain whether there exists a set of common changepoints for more than two time series. The interested reader is encouraged to examine their description of this extension.

Example of Detecting and Comparing Changepoints

In order to provide a complete worked example of changepoint detection and comparison, we will examine discipline referral data drawn from two elementary schools. For each school, the number of discipline referrals to the main office was collected for each of 120 days. The schools differed with respect to programs designed to reduce discipline issues. In School A, teachers were trained in de-escalation techniques to use with students. For School B, teachers were trained in de-escalation techniques and a dedicated staff member was present whom teachers could call on to help with discipline issues when needed. For each school, training occurred between days 57 and 60. In addition, the dedicated discipline staff member was introduced into School B on day 61. The primary research questions of interest were:

1. Was there a clear changepoint in the number of discipline referrals in each school?
2. If so, did this changepoint differ between the two schools?

Changepoint detection and changepoint detection comparisons using the methods described above were used to address these questions.

Data exploration

Prior to conducting the changepoint analysis, we will first examine a plot of the number of referrals by day for each of the schools, as in Figure 2. In addition, we have included a locally weighted regression line (LOESS) in order to provide some insights into the relationship between time and the number of referrals. Recall that the training was completed at day 60 and that the discipline specific staff member began their work on day 61. These graphs reveal a decrease in the number of referrals at each school, particularly after day 60. In addition, based on the sample data it appears that the number of referrals began to decline earlier and more markedly for School B than for School A. However, until a formal statistical comparison is made, we cannot be sure whether this apparent difference is truly present or simply an example of sample variation.

Changepoint detection

After examining the raw data, we can now assess whether there are statistically identifiable changepoints in the mean number of discipline referrals for each school and if so, where they are most likely to have occurred. Table 1 includes the number and locations of changepoints for each school. Based on these analyses, it appears that there is one changepoint in each school, at day 100 for School A and day 71 for School B. In other words, there was a statistically detectable change in the number of discipline referrals in each school. The mean number of referrals for each school before and after the changepoints also appears in Table 1. For both schools, there was a decline in the number of discipline referrals after the changepoint, as well as in the variability of these referrals. Finally, Figure 3 includes the likelihood values for all possible changepoints for each school. For each school, we can see that there is only one clear changepoint (represented by the peaks in the graph). Therefore, we can be very confident in our changepoint results.

Comparison of changepoint location

Next, we will use the Bayesian methodology described above to ascertain whether the locations of the changepoints for the two schools are significantly different. In other words, based on the changepoint detection described above, it appears that the decline in the number of discipline referrals came earlier for School B. However, it is not clear whether this apparent difference is due to random sampling variability or if it represents a true difference in changepoint location. Based on the Bayesian analysis, the *p*-value for the null hypothesis that the two schools have the same changepoint is 0.0006. Because this value is less than 0.05, we can reject the null hypothesis and conclude that the changepoint for School B occurs earlier than that for School A.

Comparison of number of referrals before and after the changepoint

Finally, now that we have identified the changepoints in the number of discipline referrals for each school and determined that they occurred at different points in time, we may also be interested in comparing the mean number of referrals for the schools before and after the changepoint. We will compare the means using a Poisson regression model, with school and time (before or after the changepoint) as the independent variables and the number of referrals as the dependent variable. We used Poisson regression in this case, rather than a more common approach such as analysis of variance, because the data are counts rather than scores. Count data is typically best analyzed using a Poisson regression model (Agresti, 2013). The results appear in Table 2. These results reveal that there was a statistically significant difference between the mean number of referrals for the schools before and after the changepoint. The rate ratio expresses the difference in the rate of discipline referrals between the schools before and after the changepoint. School B had approximately 2/3 (0.66) the number of referrals as did School A, and referrals were slightly more than 1/10 (0.13) as likely to occur after the changepoint as before it. In addition, there was a statistically significant interaction between school and changepoint. The interaction between school and time reflects the fact that the change in the number of discipline referrals appears to have declined by a larger amount for School A (11.66 to 1.55) than for School B (7.63 to 2.14). In addition, it appears that the mean number of referrals was larger across time for School A and for the period before the changepoint. The rate ratio for an interaction term is not as easily interpretable as it is for main effects.

Conclusion

The overall goal of this study was to demonstrate how researchers can examine time series data for the presence of changepoints and then compare the location of such changepoints for two or more such series. Researchers working in psychology, education, social work, or other human service sciences may be faced with situations in which measurements of two or more time series have been made, changepoints are clearly present in each, and it is of interest to ascertain whether these changepoints occurred at different locations. For example, developmental psychologists may be interested in comparing the impact that an educational intervention might have on language development for children in a classroom. The intervention may impact each child in a different way, leading to differences in the point at which language development changes. The model examined here would allow researchers to formally test the null hypothesis that the change in development occurred at the same point in time for the children in the sample. Without such a hypothesis test, researchers could only use descriptive approaches based on graphs or point estimates of change location, without the ability to make more definitive statements regarding the equality of these locations.

Finally, we will close by saying that changepoint detection is easily carried using the free software package R. The code and data associated with this example are available to readers at https://holmesfinch.substack.com/. In addition, although the current example involved a count variable, this methodology can be applied to continuous variables, such as test scores, to ordinal variables (e.g., teacher ratings of child behavior), and categorical variables (e.g., success/not success for a mathematics assessment). In addition, changepoint detection and comparison can also be carried out for more than two time series and when more than one changepoint is present in the data. Generally speaking, however, we would only be interested in comparing changepoints between time series with the same number of measurements.

Impact statement

This manuscript describes a statistical approach to detecting and comparing changes in developmental trajectories that can be very useful to researchers in early childhood, who often work with longitudinal data in which change is common and of interest.

Table 1
Number and location of changepoints for each school

School	Changepoint number	Changepoint location	Mean (SD) referrals before change	Mean (SD) referrals after change
A	1	100	11.66 (3.75)	1.55 (1.36)
B	1	71	7.63 (3.33)	2.14 (1.87)

Table 2
Poisson regression results for number of discipline referrals by school, time (before/after changepoint) and the interaction

Variable	Slope	Rate ratio	Standard error	Z	p
Intercept	2.46		0.03	88.87	<0.001
School	-0.42	0.66	0.05	-8.15	<0.001
Time	-2.02	0.13	0.18	-11.09	<0.001
SchoolXTime	0.75	2.12	0.21	3.54	<0.001

Figure 1
Examples of time series with changepoints for the mean and variance

Changepoint in the mean

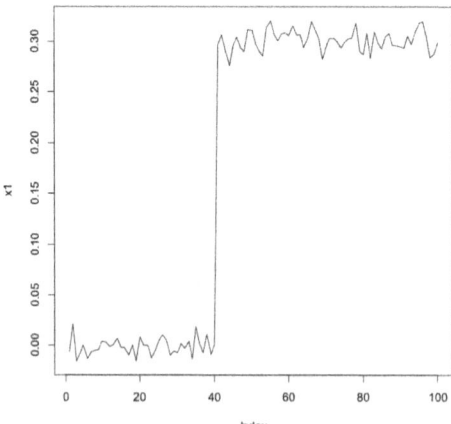

Changepoints in Developmental Trajectories 99

Figure 1 continued
Changepoint in the variance

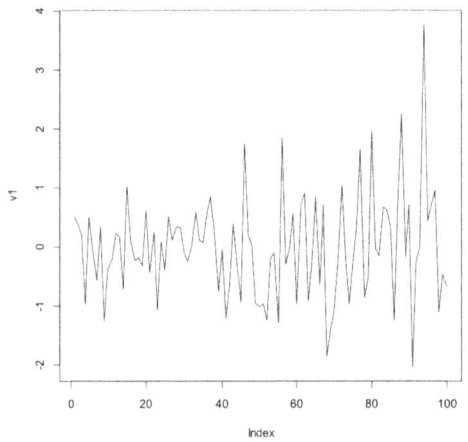

Figure 2
Number of discipline referrals with LOESS smoothed line by day for Schools A and B

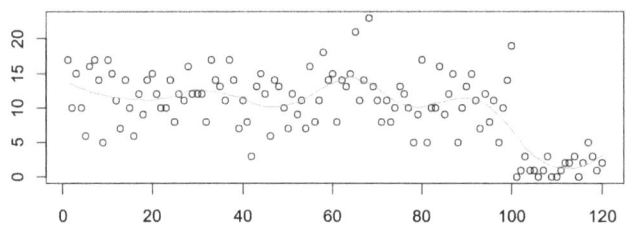

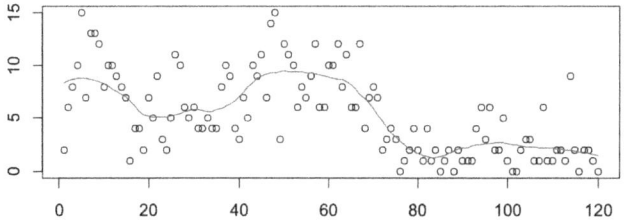

Figure 3
Likelihood values of changepoint locations for Schools A and B

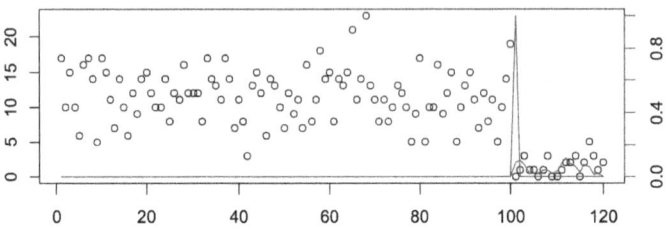

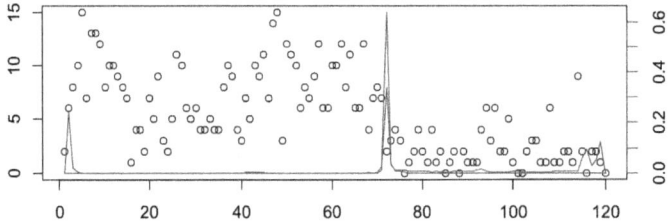

References

Agresti, A. (2013) *Categorical Data Analysis.* 3rd Edition, John Wiley & Sons Inc., Hoboken.

Aminikhanghahi, S., & Cook, D. J. (2017). A survey of methods for time series change point detection. *Knowledge and Information Systems, 51*(2), 339–367. https://doi.org/10.1007/s10115-016-0987-z

Auger, I. E., & Lawrence, C. E. (1989). Algorithms for the optimal identification of segment neighborhoods. *Bulletin of Mathematical Biology, 51*(1), 39–54. https://doi.org/10.1007/BF02458835

Carlson, S. A., Fulton, J. E., Lee, S. M., Maynard, L. M., Brown, D. R., Kohl III, H. W., & Dietz, W. H. (2008). Physical education and academic achievement in elementary school: Data from the Early Childhood Longitudinal Study. *American Journal of Public Health, 98*(4), 721–727. https://doi.org/10.2105/AJPH.2007.117176

Chen, A. Y., & Escarce, J. J. (2010). Family structure and childhood obesity, Early Childhood Longitudinal Study—Kindergarten Cohort. *Preventing Chronic Disease, 7*(3). http://www.cdc.gov/pcd/issues/2010/may/09_0156.htm. Cleynen, A., & Robin, S. (2016). Comparing change-point location in independent series. *Statistics and Computing, 26*(1-2), 263–276. https://doi.org/10.1007/s11222-014-9492-y

Eckley, I. A., Fearnhead, P., & Killick, R. (2011). Analysis of changepoint models. In D. Barber, A. T. Cemgil, & S. Chiappa (Eds.), *Bayesian time series models*. Cambridge University Press.

Edwards, A. W. F., & Cavalli-Sforza, L. L. (1965). A method for cluster analysis. *Biometrics, 21*(2), 362–375. https://doi.org/10.2307/2528096

Espinosa, L. M., Laffey, J. M., Whittaker, T., & Sheng, Y. (2006). Technology in the home and the achievement of young children: Findings from the Early Childhood Longitudinal Study. *Early Education and Development, 17*(3), 421-441. https://doi.org/10.1207/s15566935eed1703_5

Hoemann, K., Xu, F., & Barrett, L. F. (2019). Emotion words, emotion concepts, and emotional development in children: A constructionist hypothesis. *Developmental Psychology, 55*(9), 1830. https://doi.org/10.1037/dev0000686

Hušková, M., & Kirch, C. (2008). Bootstrapping confidence intervals for the change-point of time series. *Journal of Time Series Analysis, 29*(6), 947–972. https://doi.org/10.1111/j.1467-9892.2008.00589.x

Killick, R., Fearnhead, P., & Eckley, I. A. (2012). Optimal detection of changepoints with a linear computational cost. *Journal of the American Statistical Association, 107*, 1590-1598. https://doi.org/10.1080/01621459.2012.737745

Muggeo, V. M. (2003). Estimating regression models with unknown breakpoints. *Statistics in Medicine, 22*, 3055–3071. https://doi.org/10.1002/sim.1545

Rigaill, G., Lebarbier, E., & Robin, S. (2012). Exact posterior distributions and model selection criteria for multiple change-point detection problems. *Statistics and Computing, 22*, 917–929. https://doi.org/10.1007/s11222-011-9258-8

Silva, E. G., & Teixeira, A. A. C. (2008). Surveying structural change: Seminal contributions and a bibliometric account. *Structural Change and Economic Dynamics, 19*(4), 27-300. https://doi.org/10.1016/j.strueco.2008.02.001

Comparison of Multidimensional Models for Extreme Response Styles

W. Holmes Finch and Brian F. French

Abstract

Self-administered scales are ubiquitous throughout the social sciences. Therefore, it is crucial that they properly reflect the measured latent trait(s), and are not influenced by other factors. One potential threat to validity is the response style favored by an individual completing the items. In particular, a tendency to engage in extreme responding (ERS) can result in a tendency to provide responses in the outer range of the response scale, independent of the actual level of the response to the item. The purpose of this study was to demonstrate how several models can be used to account for ERS in practice, how results from these models compare to one another, and how the models can be used to understand the nature of extreme responding. A full set of results involving a scale assessing achievement goal orientation is presented, and implications for practice are discussed.

Keywords: *Response styles, Extreme responding, Item response theory trees*

Self-report scales are common in social science research for measuring many constructs. With such scales, individuals respond to rating scale items to indicate their level of agreement with a statement from a set number of options (e.g., Strongly Disagree to Strongly Agree). Collectively, the items measure a latent trait of interest (e.g., aspects of executive functioning). Some respondents demonstrate response styles characterized by a tendency to locate their ratings in a limited number of the possible options. One common case is extreme response style (ERS), in which an individual has a tendency to select options at either end of the rating scale (Bolt & Johnson, 2009), irrespective of their actual trait level. An individual's tendency to exhibit ERS is largely independent of the measured trait (e.g.,

Weijters et al., 2010). ERS can hinder score validity by altering item responses, distorting measurement of the target trait, and creating differential item functioning (Thissen-Roe & Thissen, 2013).

Self-report scales are commonly used in research with young children. Such scales are particularly effective in ascertaining teacher ratings of teacher and parent perceptions regarding children's behavior and academic performance (e.g., Casale et al., 2023; Kamphaus & Reynolds, 2015). Obtaining accurate and informative ratings is particularly important given the increased emphasis on obtaining multiple data sources and methods in the context of early childhood research (Sevön et al., 2023). This literature suggests that inclusion of perspectives from a variety of sources will help to provide a more complete picture of children's experiences (Murray, 2013). Indeed, authors have called for inclusion of the children's voices in such research (e.g., Christensen & James, 2008) with data gathered in a variety of ways using a Mosaic approach (Sevön Sevón et al; Rogers & Boyd, 2020). However, it is also important to note that perceptions, whether of the children themselves or adults in their lives, may be impacted by ERS.

Given problems caused by ERS, models accounting for its presence are recommended to obtain more accurate latent trait estimates. One such model is the multidimensional nominal response (MNRM; Bolt & Newton, 2011), which includes a latent variable for the target trait and a latent variable for ERS. The target trait estimate should reflect only the portion of the item responses that does not include ERS. A second approach involves the use of the IRTree model (Thissen-Roe & Thissen, 2013), which posits that people engage in a 2-stage response process. First, response direction (i.e., agree or disagree) is determined. Second, response intensity, or the tendency of an individual to provide extreme item responses is determined. Jin and Wang (2014) recommended using the modified generalized partial credit model (MGPCM), which treats item thresholds as random effects. This random effect reflects individual differences in the probability of providing extreme responses, even when respondents' latent trait level is the same. The purpose of the current study is to demonstrate the utility of models for ERS for adjusting scores on the primary latent trait, and to show how the results obtained from this model can be used to gain insights into the nature of extreme responding.

Response styles

As noted above, self-report scales are ubiquitous in the social sciences. They are used to measure all aspects of human psychology, including affect, personality, cognitive functioning, executive functioning, and mood, among many other traits. Given this importance, it is crucial that scores obtained from these scales reflect the target trait (e.g., depression) as accurately as possible. One potential threat to the validity of item responses comes in the form of systematic response styles (Plieninger & Meiser, 2014; Bolt & Newton, 2011). Individuals who exhibit systematic response styles have a tendency to select response options at a specific location in a Likert type response set, such as in the extremes (ERS) or in the middle of the scale (MRS or mild response style). Researchers have demonstrated that when ERS or MRS are present, person parameter estimates for the latent trait(s) of interest can be biased, thereby calling into question the validity of these scores (e.g., Thisen-Roe & Thissen, 2013) and impacting their utility in analyses with other variables (De Beuckelaer et al., 2010). Given these threats to validity, it is important that researchers assess the possible impact of ERS/MRS on scale item responses, and model it when present (Weijters et al., 2010).

A variety of models have been proposed for the purpose of characterizing ERS, and separating the response style trait from the trait associated with the primary construct of interest. Research has found that generally speaking, ERS is weakly correlated at most with the traits of interest (e.g., Jin & Wang, 2014; Bolt & Newton, 2011). In other words, the tendency to engage in extreme responding is essentially the same for individuals with differing levels of the latent traits of interest. At the same time, it is unclear whether response style is associated with specific personality traits, such as negative emotions, the likelihood to comply, or agreeableness. Addressing this issue is one focus of the current study. Next, we present a description of three models that have been demonstrated as effective tools for modeling ERS, which is the focus of the current work.

Multidimensional Nominal Response Model

One approach that has been suggested for modeling ERS is the multidimensional nominal response model (MNRM). These models are an extension of the nominal response model (NRM) described by Bock (1972). The MNRM takes the basic NRM and adds an additional dimension to account for respondents' propensity to engage in ERS. In the unidimensional case, the MNRM is written as:

$$P(U_j = k | \theta_1, \theta_{ERS}) = \frac{e^{(a_{jk1}\theta_{i1} + a_{jkERS}\theta_{iERS} + c_{jk})}}{\sum_{h=1}^{k} e^{(a_{jh1}\theta_{i1} + a_{jhERS}\theta_{iERS} + c_{jh})}} \qquad (1)$$

Where

θ_1 = Substantive trait for subject i

θ_{ERS} = ERS trait for subject i

a_{jk1} = Interval spaced category k slope for item j for substantive trait

a_{jkERS} = Interval spaced extreme category slope for item j for ERS trait

c_{jk} = Intercept parameter for category k on item j

In this context, each member of the sample has separate latent trait values for the construct of interest (e.g., depression, anxiety), and for the propensity to engage in ERS. Thus, an individual who is more likely to provide extreme responses will have larger θ_{ERS} values, separate from the value on the focal latent trait.

In order to identify the model and thereby obtain model estimates, some constraints must be placed on parameters. One common such approach is to constrain the slope category parameters (a_{jk1}) for a given trait to be constant across items (Bolt & Newton, 2011). Indeed, these values can be set to a particular value (e.g., 1) for the latent traits, thereby leading to an analog to the partial credit model (PCM). Adding this constraint allows for the estimation of correlations among the latent traits, including θ_{ERS}. These correlations can yield important insights into the nature of ERS in the population. The MNRM can be fit to the data using the Bayesian estimation framework, as will be discussed in more detail in the Methods section.

Modified Generalized Partial Credit Model (MGPCM)

An alternative approach to accounting for extreme responding focuses on the items rather than the individuals. Whereas MNRM accounts for ERS by including a latent trait specifically assessing an individual's propensity to engage in that behavior, Jin and Wang (2014) described a model that accounts for ERS through the inclusion of a random effect that is used to weight the individual item thresholds in the context of a generalized partial credit model (GPCM). A random effect refers to a measure of an individual respondent's personal item responding pattern. This model is written as

$$\frac{ln(P_{ikj})}{P_{ij(k-1)}} = a_j\theta_{i1} - (\beta_i - \omega_i\tau_{ij}) \quad (3)$$

Where

P_{ikj} = Probability of giving response k for item j by respondent i

$P_{ij(k-1)}$ = Probability of giving response j-1 for item i by respondent i

θ_i = Latent trait for respondent i

a_j = Discrimination for item j

β_j = Overall location for item j

τ_{ij} = Threshold k on item j

ω_i = Weight parameter for respondent i in the ERS dimension.

The purpose of ω_i is to control the distance between adjacent thresholds for a given item. It is assumed to follow the lognormal distribution with a mean of 0 and a variance of σ^2. Values of ω_i less than 1 yield a contracted scale (i.e., pulls item thresholds closer to the middle) meaning that extreme responses are more likely to be endorsed; i.e., a propensity to engage in ERS. In contrast, when $\omega_i > 1$, the thresholds are pushed away from the center, so that the respondent has a tendency toward MRS. Finally, respondents for whom $\omega_i = 1$ do not exhibit either ERS or MRS. As with the MNRM, each respondent has a unique propensity to engage in extreme responding as reflected in ω_i. In addition, the item discrimination parameters can be set equal to 1 for each item, thereby yielding the MPCM.

IRTree Model

A common facet of both MNRM and MGPCM is that response styles, be they ERS or MRS, are assumed to come from a latent trait associated with the individual. In the case of MNRM, this trait is a full blown latent variable that is modeled in the same way as are the constructs of interest. For MGPCM, person-specific latent variables associated with each respondent adjust the location of the item thresholds for that person. The IRTree approach (Thissen-Roe & Thissen, 2013) to modeling response styles focuses on the response process itself, and incorporates that information into an additional latent trait associated with each respondent. In the IRTree framework, responding to Likert type items is assumed to consist of a 2-stage process. In the first stage, the respondent chooses the general direction of their response (e.g., agree or disagree). In the second stage, the individual makes a decision regarding the intensity of their response. The direction of the response is taken to be a function of the measured trait (e.g., mood, personality) whereas the intensity of the response is assumed to come from a second trait measuring the propensity of ERS. In the IRTree framework, the degree of response intensity is assumed to be independent of the response direction. In other words, the likelihood of an individual engaging in ERS is not related to their location on the trait of interest.

IRTree model parameters are estimated using two separate sets of 2-parameter logistic (2PL) IRT models, one for the direction and the other for intensity. Direction is modeled as:

$$P(D_1 = 1 | \theta_1) = \frac{1}{1+e^{-(b_1 \pm a_1 \theta_1)}} \quad (5)$$

And

$$P(D_1 = 0 | \theta_1) = 1 - \frac{1}{1+e^{-(b_1 \pm a_1 \theta_1)}} \quad (6)$$

Where

$D_1 = 1 =$ Agree

$D_1 = 0 =$ Disagree

$\theta_1 =$ Latent trait of interest

$b_1 =$ Threshold for item on trait of interest (e.g., Disagree versus Agree)

$a_1 =$ Discrimination parameter for item on latent trait of interest

The second portion of the decision process involving intensity is then modeled using the following models.

$$P(D_2 = 1 | \theta_{ERS}, \theta_1) = \frac{1}{1+e^{-(b_2 + a_2 \theta_{ERS} + va_2(b_1 + a_1 \theta_1))}} \quad (7)$$

And

$$P(D_2 = 1 | \theta_{ERS}, \theta_1) = 1 - \frac{1}{1+e^{-(b_2 + a_2 \theta_{ERS} + va_2(b_1 + a_1 \theta_1))}} \quad (8)$$

Where

$D_2 = 1 =$ Strong intensity response

$D_2 = 0 =$ Non-strong intensity response

$\theta_{ERS} =$ Latent trait for extreme response style

$b_2 =$ Threshold for item on extreme response style latent trait (Strong versus Weak)

$a_2 =$ Discrimination parameter for item on extreme response style latent trait

v = Parameter introducing compensatory nature of the latent traits

The term $va_2(b_1+a_1\theta_1)$ is a shift parameter that is additive for response options above the midpoint (e.g., K=3 or 4) and subtractive for options below the midpoint (e.g., K=1 or 2). The IRTree model can be expanded to account for more any number of response options. If there are more than 4 such values, then the direction of response is modeled using the 2PL model, and the intensity is measured using the graded response model.

Study Goal

The goal of this study was to demonstrate the use of MNRM, IRTree, and MPCM, for exploring the nature ERS for a particular scale and the subsequent post-modeling follow-up analyses. Such investigations have a great deal of potential utility in social science research, both because they can yield estimates of the primary trait of interest adjusted for ERS, and also because exploring the nature of ERS provides insights into extreme responding behavior for individuals who are administered these scales. Therefore, our goal was to demonstrate how these ERS models can be used in this context, what the resulting parameter estimates reveal about response styles, and how the latent traits can be used to gain insights into respondent behavior.

Methodology

In order to address the goals of this study, the PCM, MPCM, MNRM, and IRTree models were fit to data gathered from a sample of 432 college undergraduates. The students were part of a larger study in which instruments measuring a variety of personality traits were administered. Among other measures, the participants completed items on the Adult Temperament Questionnaire (ATQ; Evans & Rothbart, 2007), which includes subscales measuring negative affect, effortful control, and orienting sensitivity. In addition, participants were given the multidimensional perfectionism scale (MPS; Hewitt & Flett, 2004), and the Achievement Goal Questionnaire (AGQ; Elliot

& Murayama, 2008). The study participants were also asked to read 4 brief descriptions of parent-child interactions and then to select the one that best reflected their own experience. These responses were then used to classify each participant as having either a secure or an insecure parental attachment.

The focal analysis for this study involved fitting the PCM, MPCM, MNRM, and IRTree models to the 12 items that make up the AGQ. These items, which appear in Table 1, measure the nature of the goals underlying respondents' desire to achieve academic success. Item responses take the form of Strongly Disagree, Disagree, Agree, and Strongly Agree to each of the statements. The standard PCM was fit with R software, version 4.02 (R Core Team, 2020) using a marginal maximum likelihood estimator with the ltm library. The expected a posteriori estimates from this approach were used as the latent trait estimate for achievement goal motivation. The MPCM, MNRM, and IRTree models were fit to the data with a Bayesian estimator using SAS, version 9.4 (SAS Institute, 2019). For each model, 2 chains were used, with each being 20,000 links long. The first 10,000 replications in each chain served as the burn-in period, with the second 10,000 data points being used to obtain the parameter estimates. Parameter convergence was assessed using the potential scale reduction (PSR) statistic. Across parameters and models, PSR values were below 1.01, indicating convergence (Kaplan, 2014).

Table 1
Item threshold estimates for standard PCM model

Item	c1	c2	c3
1: My goal is to completely master the material presented in my classes	-1.45	-0.39	1.04
2: I want to avoid learning less than it is possible to learn	-0.18	0.13	1.08
3: It is important for me to do better than other students	-0.60	-0.20	0.52

Table 1 continued

Item	c1	c2	c3
4: I want to avoid performing poorly compared to others	-1.13	-1.12	-0.42
5: I want to learn as much as possible	-2.24	-0.70	-0.40
6: It is important for me to avoid an incomplete understanding of the course material	-1.35	-0.38	0.56
7: It is important for me to understand the content of my courses as thoroughly as possible	-1.66	-0.60	0.51
8: My goal is to avoid performing worse than other students	0.38	-0.40	0.45
9: I want to do well compared to other students	-1.22	-0.48	-0.13
10: It is important for me to avoid doing poorly compared to other students	-0.46	-0.41	-0.05
11: My goal is to perform better than the other students	0.16	0.16	0.36
12: My goal is to avoid learning less than I possibly could	-0.21	0.03	0.88

In order to gain insights into the nature of ERS behavior, several analyses were conducted. For each fitted model, item parameter estimates were obtained. In addition, trait estimates for study participants were correlated with one another and with the personality measures discussed above. These correlations provided insights into the nature of extreme responding in terms of various aspects of personality. Mean scores on the ERS traits derived from MPCM, MNRM, and IRTree were compared using an independent samples t-test, employing the Bonferroni correction. In addition, Cohen's *d* was used to characterize the mean differences. Finally, the relationship between the primary trait of interest (achievement goal orientation) and college grade point average (GPA) was assessed using Pearson's correlation coefficient. Of particular interest were differences in the correlation between achievement GPA and achievement goal orientation as characterized by the naïve PCM estimate, and the primary trait estimates from MNRM, MPCM, and IRTree. Differences in these correlations would reflect the impact of distilling the primary trait of interest from the effects of ERS. The computer code and example data are available at https://holmesfinch.substack.com/.

Results

Item parameter estimates

The item threshold estimates for the 12 items in the AGS appear in Table 1. Based on these results, it appears that items 5 ("I want to learn as much as possible") and 9 ("I want to do well compared to other students") were the easiest for respondents to endorse. This determination is based on the threshold values of -2.24, -0.70, and -0.40 and -1.22, -0.48, and -0.13. In addition, the first threshold for item 1 ("My goal is to completely master the material presented in my classes") was very low, meaning that it was unlikely for respondents to strongly disagree with this statement. On the other hand, the third threshold for this item was the second largest, indicating that students were relatively unlikely to strongly agree. A similar pattern was evident for item 7 ("It is important for me to understand the content of my courses as thoroughly as possible"), particularly for the first threshold. None of the other items had thresholds above 1, indicating that they were relatively easy to endorse either agree or strongly agree.

Table 2 displays the MPCM threshold and location parameters for the 12 AGS items. Of particular note is the shift in thresholds for items 1, 4, 5, 6, and 7 when the response style trait was included in the model. For items 1, 6, and 7, the first and third thresholds became more extreme, meaning that it was less likely that respondents would select either Strongly Disagree or Strongly Agree; i.e., after accounting for response style respondents the moderate response options (Agree or Disagree) were the most likely to be selected. The thresholds for items 4 and 5 were shifted in a positive direction for the MPCM as compared to the PCM. This result indicates that after accounting for the ERS trait, respondents were generally less likely to express agreement with these items.

Table 2
Item threshold estimates for standard MPCM response styles model

Item	B	Tau1	Tau2	Tau3
1	-0.90	-3.08	-0.24	3.32
2	1.13	-0.84	-0.18	1.02
3	-0.09	-0.51	-0.01	0.52
4	-0.78	-0.45	-0.04	0.49
5	-3.50	-1.20	0.07	1.13
6	-1.19	-2.02	-0.09	2.11
7	-1.84	-2.50	-0.26	2.76
8	0.09	-0.34	-0.11	0.45
9	-0.48	-0.54	0.00	0.54
10	-0.27	-0.44	-0.02	0.46
11	0.19	-0.36	-0.05	0.41
12	0.65	-0.68	-0.30	0.98

Table 3 includes the threshold parameter estimates for the MNRM. The intercepts for Strongly Disagree were lowest for items 4, 5, and 7 suggesting that they were the most difficult for respondents to strongly disagree with. At the same time, items 4 and 5 had the largest intercepts for Strongly Agree, meaning that they were also the most difficult for respondents to select this category. Thus, when the MNRM is fit to the data, the Disagree and Agree response options were the most likely to be selected. In contrast, the pattern of intercepts for items 2, 3, 8, 11, and 12 were such that the extreme responses (Strongly Disagree and Strongly Agree) were more likely to be selected than was the case for the other items.

Table 3
Item parameter estimates for MNRM response styles model

Item	c1	c2	c3	c4
1	-1.41	0.65	1.09	-0.33
2	-0.46	0.12	0.12	0.22
3	-0.64	0.3	0.52	-0.18
4	-1.83	-0.38	0.88	1.33
5	-2.57	0.2	1.01	1.36
6	-1.41	0.46	0.88	0.07
7	-1.81	0.42	1.08	0.31
8	0.09	-0.13	0.27	-0.23
9	-1.5	0.12	0.67	0.71
10	-0.77	-0.05	0.41	0.41
11	0.13	0.21	0.07	-0.41
12	-0.08	0.42	0.37	-0.71

Table 4 includes the IRTree item parameter estimates. Of particular interest are the thresholds for the direction and strength aspects of the items. Based on the fact that the largest threshold on the agreement parameter was 0.27, we can conclude that none of the items proved to be very difficult with which to agree. Items 4, 9, and 10 had the most strongly negative thresholds for the agreement parameter, meaning that they were the most difficult for respondents to disagree with. With respect to the intensity of response, the majority of the items had negative thresholds, suggesting that it is relatively easy for respondents to provide an intense response to these items. The notable exception to this finding was item 4, which had an intensity of response threshold value of 1. In contrast, items 8 and 11 had the smallest threshold for this trait, so that providing a strong response to them is relatively easy; i.e., requires lower values of the latent trait.

Table 4
Item parameter estimates for IRTree response styles model

Item	A1	B1	A2	B2	Nu
1	0.39	-0.42	0.44	-0.67	-0.01
2	0.38	0.27	0.18	-0.06	-0.08
3	2.99	-0.80	1.43	-0.78	0.33
4	3.03	-3.04	2.64	1.00	0.01
5	0.20	-1.15	0.48	-0.32	-1.84
6	0.39	-0.52	0.46	-0.36	-0.42
7	0.38	-0.75	0.54	-0.48	-0.69
8	4.59	-0.91	2.19	-1.24	0.36
9	5.71	-3.50	3.52	0.43	0.03
10	7.39	-3.29	3.22	0.27	0.06
11	4.81	-0.39	1.54	-1.47	0.48
12	0.51	-0.03	0.42	-0.07	2.22

ERS Trait Estimates

Figure 1 includes boxplots for the latent trait estimates produced by each of the models considered in this study. For the PCM, MPCM, and MNRM estimates the median of the sample is near 0, which is as anticipated, given the assumption of a standard normal distribution for the trait. The means and medians of the IRTree parameter estimates were slightly negative, in contrast. Finally, the standard deviations for the MPCM ERS, and the two MNRM traits were lower than those of the other latent traits.

The Pearson's correlation coefficients between the standard PCM trait estimate and the estimates derived from the MPCM, MNRM, and IRTree models appear in Table 5. The PCM trait was significantly positively correlated with the primary (not ERS) traits for MPCM and MNRM, as well as both the IRTree direction and strength traits. On the other hand, the MPCM and MNRM ERS traits were not significantly correlated with the PCM trait estimate.

Figure 1
Boxplots, means, and standard deviations of the PCM, MPCM, MNRM, and IRTree latent trait estimates

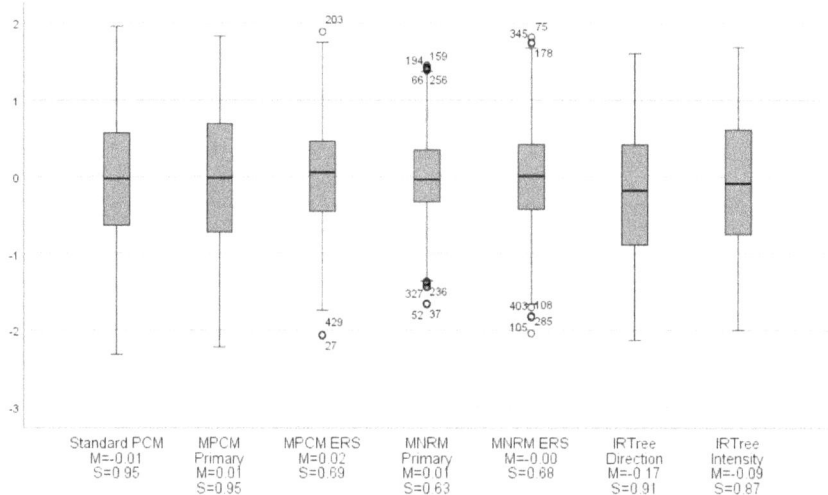

Table 5
Pearson's correlation coefficients between standard PCM latent trait and ERS models parameter estimates

Trait estimate	Pearson's r with PCM estimate
MPCM primary trait	0.88*
MPCM ERS	-0.03
MNRM primary trait	0.82*
MNRM ERS	-0.01
IRTree direction	0.86*
IRTree strength	0.55*

Note: *Statistically significant at α = 0.05.

The Pearson correlation coefficients among the MNRM, MPCM, and IRTree trait estimates appear in Table 6. From these results, we can see that the MPCM and MNRM primary traits are positively significantly correlated with one another, and with the IRTree traits. The relationship with the IRTree direction trait was more than twice as large as that for the intensity trait. The MPCM and MNRM ERS traits were not significantly correlated with any of the other traits.

Table 6
Pearson's correlation coefficients between standard PCM latent trait and ERS models parameter estimates

Trait estimate	MPCM primary	MPCM ERS	MNRM primary	MNRM ERS	IRTree direction	IRTree strength
MPCM primary trait	1	-0.03	0.84*	-0.06	0.98*	0.43*
MPCM ERS		1	-0.02	0.42*	-0.02	0.53*
MNRM primary trait			1	-0.02	0.83*	0.48*
MNRM ERS				1	0.01	0.66*
IRTree direction					1	0.06
IRTree strength						1

Relationships Between ERSTtrait Estimates and Scholastic Performance

In order to assess the impact of separately modeling ERS and the primary trait of interest, the Pearson's correlation coefficients relating college GPA to the PCM based achievement goal trait, as well as the achievement goal traits obtained from MPCM and MNRM, after ERS have been modeled separately. These results revealed that the relationship between the PCM trait estimate and GPA was 0.15 and statistically significant, indicating a weak positive relationship between being more achievement goal oriented and actual academic performance. When ERS is modeled separately from the trait of interest, the correlation between the primary achievement goal trait and GPA was 0.27 for MNRM, and 0.26 for MPCM. In other words, when the achievement goal trait is separated from response style, the relationship with GPA increased in value. The correlations between GPA and IRTree direction was 0.32 (statistically significant), and 0.11 (not statistically significant) with intensity. These results suggest that individuals who tended to agree with the achievement goal items had higher GPAs, but that the intensity of these feelings were not associated with academic performance.

Relationships between ERS trait estimates and personality variable scores

In order to understand the nature of the ERS traits, estimates for each were correlated with scores on personality scale scores. The Pearson *r* values appear in Table 7. The pattern of correlation estimates for the MPCM and MNRM ERS trait estimates were generally comparable to one another. Specifically, both traits had statistically significant positive correlations with scores on Negative Affect, Neuroticism, and all three types of perfectionism. Taken together, these results indicate that individuals who engaged in extreme responding on the AGS reported more negative emotions, had a higher degree of neuroticism, and also had higher levels of perfectionism in terms of their school work.

Table 7
Pearson's correlation coefficients between ERS parameter estimates and personality measure scores

Personality scale	MPCM ERS	MNRM ERS	IRTree direction	IRTree strength
Negative Affect	0.20*	0.16*	-0.17*	0.12
Effortful Control	0.12	0.10	0.08	0.08
Extraversion	0.01	0.08	0.00	0.00

Table 7 continued

Personality scale	MPCM ERS	MNRM ERS	IRTree direction	IRTree strength
Orienting Sensitivity	0.09	0.04	0.09	0.07
Conformity	0.12	0.11	0.21*	-0.04
Agreeableness	-0.06	0.04	0.52*	0.41*
Conscientiousness	0.04	0.05	0.14*	0.18*
Neuroticism	0.41*	0.32*	0.02	0.05
Openness	0.09	0.12	0.08	0.13
Self-oriented	0.35*	0.41*	0.36*	0.26*
Other-oriented	0.21*	0.19*	0.21*	0.18*
Socially prescribed	0.18*	0.13*	0.20*	0.22*

Note: *Statistically significant at α = 0.05.

The IRTree direction trait (Table 7) had a statistically significant negative relationship with Negative Affect, and significant positive correlations with scores on Conformity, Agreeableness, Conscientiousness, and all three types of perfectionism. The IRTree intensity trait was significantly positively correlated with Agreeableness, Conscientiousness, and all three types of perfectionism. Therefore, individuals who were more likely to agree with a statement had lower negative emotions, and at the same time were more likely to conform to others' expectations, to have an agreeable personality, to be more conscientious, as well as more perfectionistic. Individuals who tended to provide stronger responses were also more agreeable, conscientious, and perfectionistic, as compared to those who had a tendency to provide weaker responses to the items.

Table 8 includes the means and standard deviations for the ERS traits by parental attachment status. As noted in the methods section, the means were compared between groups using an independent *t*-test, and mean differences were characterized by Cohen's *d*. There were statistically significant mean differences between the groups for the MPCM ERS, MNRM ERS, and IRTree intensity traits. In each case, the individuals who characterized their parental relationships as being secure had lower mean ERS and IRTree direction means than did those with insecure attachments. Based on commonly used guidelines for interpreting *d* (Cohen, 1988), these group mean differences would be characterized as small in magnitude. There were not statistically significant differences in the IRTree direction means between the secure and insecure attachment groups.

Table 8
Mean (standard deviation) of ERS estimates by attachment to parents, and Cohen's d for mean comparison

	Secure Mean (SD)	Insecure Mean (SD)	Cohen's *d**
MPCM ERS	-0.25 (0.88)	0.12 (0.95)	-0.26*
MNRM ERS	-0.11 (0.56)	0.05 (0.65)	-0.40*
IRTree direction	-0.22 (0.83)	-0.05 (0.90)	-0.20
IRTree intensity	-0.44 (0.80)	-0.05 (0.91)	-0.43*

Note: *Statistically significant at $\alpha = 0.0125$.

Discussion

ERS has been shown to deleteriously impact latent trait estimation with factor analysis and item response theory (Thissen-Roe & Thissen, 2013). Thus, when ERS is not properly accounted for, the estimates of the primary latent traits of interest (e.g., academic achievement, cognitive ability, mood, personality, executive functioning) may not accurately reflect what they are intended to measure. This issue is particularly problematic because such scores are often used to make important decisions about individuals. The purpose of the current study was to demonstrate how models for ERS can be used to both correct person parameter estimates, and to gain insights into the nature of extreme responding itself. These models can be fit using standard available software, and the parameter estimates can be saved and used in subsequent analyses, as shown here.

The results of this study illustrated the importance of correcting latent trait estimates. Specifically, when the effects of ERS were separated from the estimates of the target latent trait (achievement goal orientation in this case), the correlations with academic performance increased in value. Given that theory would suggest a positive relationship between achievement goal orientation and academic performance (e.g., Chen & Wong, 2015), this difference in results between the naïve and ERS corrected estimates is important. Were a researcher to ignore the potential impact of ERS, they would conclude that the relationship between achievement goal orientation and college GPA was weak and not statistically significant. However, when ERS was accounted for, the correlation coefficient with the achievement goal trait nearly doubled in value, and more clearly conformed to theoretical expectations.

In addition to demonstrating the importance of adjusting the target trait for the propensity of respondents to engage in ERS, this study also demonstrated how researchers can gain insights into extreme responding behavior itself. Specifically, individuals who were more likely to engage in extreme responding also exhibited more negative emotions, a higher degree of neuroticism, greater perfectionism, and less secure attachment to their parents. In addition, respondents who were more likely to agree with statements based on the IRTree model parameter estimates were generally more agreeable, conscientious, conforming, and perfectionistic than were those who were less likely to agree.

Directions for future research

The study reported here represents a thorough examination of the results obtained using the MPCM, MNRM, and IRTree models. As noted above, they demonstrate the utility of these models for both adjusting estimates of the primary latent trait of interest, and for more thoroughly understanding differences between individuals who are more likely to engage in ERS a those who are less likely to do so. We recognize, however, that this is but a single study using one sample of data. Thus, future work should investigate similar questions using other data sources and scales. In addition, the models fit to the data in this study included only a single latent trait of interest. However, the MPCM, MNRM, and IRTree models can all be extended to the case of a multidimensional latent structure. Thus, future work should examine with both empirical and simulated data how these models work in terms of parameter recovery. Finally, future research should examine the question of differential item functioning (DIF) with respect to the item parameters in the model. It is well known that the presence of DIF can impact the validity of scales (Gòmez-Benito et al., 2018), just as can ERS. Thus, it would seem likely that the combination of DIF and ERS together would negatively affect the performance of scales such as those commonly used in the social sciences. Methods for investigating DIF in the presence of ERS would, therefore, seem to be an important issue for future research.

Conclusions

Researchers need to be aware of the potential impact of ERS on item responses. The current study, as well as previous work, has demonstrated that when ERS is present, the behavior of scales, in the form of correlations with other scale scores for example, may well be impacted. Therefore, when it is anticipated that ERS is potentially present, it is important for these effects to be modeled and removed from the estimates of the trait(s) of interest. In addition, it was demonstrated that insight into the nature of ERS behavior can be informative in and of itself. For the current dataset, there was a variety of relationships between a propensity to engage in ERS and a variety of personality measures. Thus, researchers can gain a better understanding of respondent behavior by investigating relationships between ERS and personality and demographic variables. In short, the current study has demonstrated that ERS is an important issue in item responding, and one which researchers should not ignore.

Impact statement

This manuscript describes a statistical approach to detecting and modeling extreme responding in surveys and tests. These methods can be very useful to researchers in early childhood, who often work with ratings of child behavior and other traits by parents and teachers.

References

Bock, R. D. (1972). Estimating item parameters and latent ability when responses are scored in two or more nominal categories. *Psychometrika, 37*, 29-51. https://doi.org/10.1007/BF02291411

Bolt, D. M., & Newton, J. R. (2011). Multiscale measurement of extreme response style. *Educational and Psychological Measurement, 71*(5), 814-833. https://doi.org/10.1177/0013164410388411

Casale, G., Herzog, M., & Volpe, R. J. (2023). Measurement efficiency of a teacher rating scale to screen students at risk for social, emotional, and behavioral problems. *Journal of Intelligence, 11*(3), 1-16. https://doi.org/10.3390/jintelligence11030057

Chen, W.-W., & Wong, Y.-L. (2015). The relationship between goal orientation and academic achievement in Hong Kong: The role of context. *The Asia-Pacific Education Researcher, 24*, 169-176. https://doi.org/10.1007/s40299-013-0169-7

Christensen, P., & James, A. (2008). *Research with children. Perspectives and practices (2nd ed).* Routledge.

Cohen, J. (1988). *Statistical power analysis for the behavioral sciences.* Routledge Academic.

De Beuckelaer, A., Weijters, B., & Rutten, A. (2010). Using ad hoc measures for response styles: A cautionary note. *Quality & Quantity: International Journal of Methodology, 44*(4), 761–775. https://doi.org/10.1007/s11135-009-9225-z

Elliot, A. J., & Murayama, K. (2008). On the measurement of achievement goals: Critique, illustration, and application. *Journal of Educational Psychology, 100*, 613–628. https://doi.org/10.1037/0022-0663.100.3.613

Evans, D. E., & Rothbart, M. K. (2007). Development of a model for adult temperament. *Journal of Research in Personality, 41*, 868-888. https://doi.org/10.1016/j.jrp.2006.11.002

Gòmez-Benito, J., Sireci, S., Padilla, Josè-Luis, Hidalgo, M. D., & Benítez, I. (2018). Differential item functioning: Beyond validity evidence based on internal structure. *Psicothema, 30*(1), 104-109. https://doi.org/10.7334/psicothema2017.183

Hewitt, P. L., & Flett, G. L. (2004). *Multidimensional Perfectionism Scale (MPS): Technical manual*. Multi-Health Systems.

Huang, H.-Y. (2016). Mixture random-effect IRT models for controlling extreme response style on rating scales. *Frontiers in Psychology, 7*, 1706. https://doi.org/10.3389/fpsyg.2016.01706

Jin, K.-Y., & Wang, W.-C. (2014). Generalized IRT models for extreme response style. *Educational and Psychological Measurement, 74*(1), 116-138. https://doi.org/10.1177/0013164413498876

Kamphaus, R. W., & Reynolds, C. R. (2015). *BASC-3 behavioral and emotional screening system*. NCS Pearson Inc.

Kaplan, D. (2014). *Bayesian statistics for the social sciences*. The Guilford Press.

Lenthal, B. C., & Stone, C. A. (2018). Bayesian analysis of multidimensional item response theory models: A discussion and illustration of three response style models. *Measurement: Interdisciplinary Research and Perspectives, 16*(2), 114-128.

Murray, J. M. (2013). Young children's research behavior? Children aged four to eight years finding solutions at home and at school. *Early Child Development and Care, 183*(8), 1147–1165. https://doi.org/10.1080/03004430.2013.792255

Plieninger, H., & Meiser, T. (2014). Validity of multiprocess IRT models for separating content and response styles. *Educational and Psychological Measurement, 74*(5), 875-899. https://doi.org/10.1177/0013164413514998

R Core Team. (2017). *R: A language and environment for statistical computing*. R Foundation for Statistical Computing.

Rogers, M., & Boyd, W. (2020). Meddling with mosaic: Reflections and adaptations. *European Early Childhood Education Research Journal, 28*(5), 642–658. https://doi.org/10.1080/1350293x.2020.1817236

SAS Institute. (2019). *SAS software, Version 9.4*. SAS Institute.

Sevón, E., Mustola, M., Sippainen, A., & Vlasov, J. (2023). Participatory research methods with young children: A systematic literature review. *Educational Review*, 1-19. https://doi.org/10.1080/00131911.2023.2215465

Thissen-Roe, A., & Thissen, D. (2013). A two-decision model for responses to Likert-type items. *Journal of Educational and Behavioral Statistics, 38*(5), 522-547. https://www.jstor.org/stable/41999438

Weijters, B., Geuens, M., & Schillewaert, N. (2010). The individual consistency of acquiescence and extreme response style in self-report questionnaires. *Applied Psychological Measurement, 34*(2), 105-121. https://doi.org/10.1177/0146621609338593

Latent Transition Analysis: A Statistical Method for Identifying Underlying Subgroups over Time

W. Holmes Finch

Abstract

Researchers working in early childhood research are often interested in assessing change over time in multiple variables. In addition, they may wish to ascertain whether there exist subgroups in the data with respect to these variables, and whether/how membership in these groups is related. Latent transition analysis (LTA) provides such researchers with a useful tool for investigating questions around such groups, including their composition, frequency, and the likelihood of moving from one to another at different points in time. The purpose of this manuscript is to provide a full demonstration of LTA and show how it can be used to examine such questions with longitudinal data. In addition to the demonstration, computer code and example data are available for readers.

A common research scenario in education, psychology, and other social sciences involves examining change in one or more phenomena over time (e.g., Bosnic et al., 2019). This framework is particularly the case for researchers working with young children, in which physical, psychological, and cognitive development tends to occur very quickly (e.g., Duchnowski et al., 2013; Remmers et al., 2014; Suades-Gonzales et al., 2017;). There exists a variety of statistical tools for researchers interested in understanding change over time, including repeated measures analysis of variance, growth curve modeling, and time series analysis. In some cases, a researcher may be interested in identifying groups within the data that differ based upon observed measurements. For example, it may be theorized that there are subgroups of preschool children based upon different trajectories in meeting developmental milestones at multiple points in time. When the number and makeup of these subgroups is not known ahead of time, researchers may use a set of statistical tools known collectively as mixture models. Such techniques can be used to focus on a single point in time or changes across two or more time points. The focus of this manuscript is on latent transition analysis (LTA), a statistical method designed to identify such unobserved (latent) subgroups based on a set of sample data. First, we will discuss latent class analysis (LCA), which is used to identify subgroups for a single time point. Next, we will extend the latent class model to multiple time points. We will then walk through a full example demonstrating how to conduct a basic LTA from beginning to end, after which we will discuss some interesting extensions that allow for assessing trait and state effects on individuals, as well as inclusion of predictor variables of subgroup membership.

As a motivating example for discussion, we consider a study in which 500 students were assessed on whether they have reached each of 5 linguistic milestones: Understands "same" versus "different," understands "on" versus "under," can use 3-word sentences, uses words that are 75% understandable by strangers, and can tell stories (American Academy of Pediatrics, 2019). The assessments were made within one month after each child's third birthday, and again 6 months later. The data were coded as '0' (did not reach the milestone) or '1' (the child did reach the milestone). If the researcher is interested in identifying latent subgroups based upon the pattern of meeting (or not) the developmental milestones at a single time point (e.g. at 3 years of age), LCA would be an appropriate tool. This analysis is extended by LTA through identification of latent classes at each time point and then estimating relationships between the groups at the two ages. These data, which were simulated, are available to readers at https://holmesfinch.substack.com/. The computer programs used for the analyses featured in this manuscript are also available at this website.

Latent Class Analysis

Prior to our discussion of LTA we will first consider LCA, which is used for identifying latent classes for a single time point. Figure 1 shows a latent class model with 5 measured variables, V1, V2, V3, V4, and V5, which can be either categorical or continuous, and a single latent variable consisting of a small number of categories. LCA was first introduced in the late 1960's by Lazarsfeld and Henry (1968) and is typically conducted in an exploratory manner, in which researchers consider several possible solutions and then select the one that provides the best statistical fit to the data and that is conceptually coherent. Researchers using LCA may have fairly firm a priori hypotheses regarding the number and nature of the latent classes underlying the data but little prior evidence supporting a definitive result, or only some general ideas about how many and what types of classes exist in the population (Collins & Lanza, 2010). In either case, exploratory use of LCA would be appropriate. When using LCA in such an exploratory manner, the researcher would fit several models to the data, each being differentiated from the others by the number of latent classes. The relative fits of these models to the data are then compared with one another in order to identify the optimal number of classes. Such fit comparisons can be made in multiple ways. One approach involves the use of the Akaike Information Criterion (AIC), the Bayesian Information Criterion (BIC), and the sample size adjusted BIC (aBIC). These statistics measure how far the model-predicted values of the observed variables are from the actual values, with a penalty for the complexity of the model added in; i.e. the number of latent classes being estimated. Smaller values of these information indices reflect better fitting models. Therefore, in practice the researcher using LCA will compare the AIC, BIC, and aBIC across the models and select the one with the smallest value as being optimal. In addition, the Bootstrap Likelihood Ratio test (BLRT; McLachlan & Peel, 2000; Nylund et al., 2007) is also useful for determining the number of latent classes to retain. This test compares the fit of a model with *k* latent classes to the fit of the model with *k*-1 latent classes, with the null hypothesis being that the two models fit the data equally well. Therefore, if the test is statistically significant, the researcher would conclude that the model with more classes is preferable to the one with fewer classes. In addition to relying on such statistical assessments of model fit, the researcher must also consider the substantive coherence of the latent classes when selecting a model (Bauer & Curran, 2004). That is, the final LCA solution must be defensible based on the types of individuals that have been grouped together, with regard to their responses on the indicators used in the analysis, as well as other potentially pertinent variables, such as demographic characteristics.

Figure 1
Latent class model with 5 observed variables

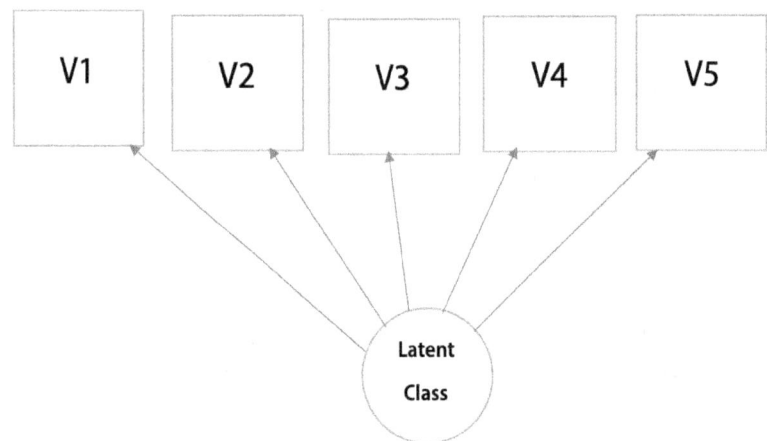

The standard LCA model linking a set of observed variables, X, with the latent class variable, Y, describes the relationship between latent class membership and the response pattern to the observed variables as:

$$\pi_{1,2,3\ldots jk}^{X_1 X_2 X_3\ldots X_j, Y} = \sum_k^K \pi_k^Y \prod \pi_{jk}^{X_j|Y} \qquad (1)$$

Where

π_{jk}^Y = Probability that a randomly selected individual will be in class k of latent variable Y

$\pi^{X|Y}$ = Probability that a member of latent class k will provide a particular response to observed indicator j

The model in Equation (1) asserts that responses to the observed variables are independent of one another given a particular latent class in Y (Goodman, 2002). This basic LCA model is characterized by two types of parameters: (a) the probability of a particular response for an observed variable conditional on latent class membership, and (b) the probability of being in a specific latent class, k, both of which will be important in interpreting the results of the model.

Basic LCA Example

We will demonstrate the conduct of LCA with the Mplus software package (Muthèn & Muthèn, 2022) using the Time 1 data from the example described above. Recall that the variables reflect whether a child has reached each of 5 developmental milestones and is coded as yes (1) or no (0). We fit models for 2, 3, and 4 latent classes and then compare fit statistics, which appear in Table 1. Lower values for the AIC, BIC, and aBIC indicate better fitting models. The BLRT compares the fit of the model with k classes (e.g., 2 classes) with the fit of the model with k-1 classes (e.g., 1 class). The null hypothesis is that the models provide equivalent fit to the data, so that a statistically significant result () means that the models provide different degrees of fit to the data. Based on the results in Table 1, we would conclude that the 3-class model yields the best fit to the data. We reach this conclusion because the 3-class model provided significantly better fit than the 2-class model ($p=0.03$), but the 4-class model did not provide significantly better fit than the 3-class model ($p=0.50$). In addition, the AIC, BIC, and aBIC values were smallest for the 3-class model.

Table 1
Latent class analysis fit statistics for Times 1 and 2

Latent classes	AIC	BIC	aBIC	LRT bootstrap p
Time 1				
2	3316.18	3362.54	3327.63	<0.0001
3	3311.64	3383.29	3329.33	0.03
4	3316.77	3413.70	3340.70	0.50
Time 2				
2	3301.56	3347.92	3313.00	<0.0001
3	3294.90	3366.55	3312.59	<0.0001
4	3301.83	3398.76	3325.76	0.51

The probabilities of achieving the developmental milestones for each class appear in Table 2. Latent class 1 was characterized by having the highest probabilities for achieving the developmental milestones in Time 1. Indeed, the probabilities were greater than 0.5 for each milestone. Therefore, we will label this latent class as "Likely to achieve all developmental milestones." Individuals in latent class 2 were likely to achieve the milestones "Uses 3- word sentences," "Uses words 75% of non-family can understand," and "Can tell stories." However, they were unlikely to achieve the developmental milestones "Understands same and different" and "Understands on and under." Given this pattern of milestone achievements, we will label this class "Likely to achieve three developmental milestones." Finally, latent class 3 was characterized by having milestone achievement probabilities of 0.30 or lower. Thus, we will label this group "Unlikely to achieve any developmental milestones."

Table 2
Probability that developmental milestone reached by latent class for Times 1 and 2

Item	Time 1	Time 2
Class 1: Likely to achieve all developmental milestones		
Understands same/different	0.58	0.57
Understands on/under	0.66	1.00
Uses 3-word sentences	0.74	0.81
Uses words 75% understood	0.72	0.76
Can tell stories	0.75	0.83
Class 2: Likely to achieve three developmental milestones		
Understands same/different	0.58	0.57
Understands on/under	0.66	1.00
Uses 3-word sentences	0.74	0.81
Uses words 75% understood	0.72	0.76
Can tell stories	0.75	0.83
Class 3: Unlikely to achieve any developmental milestones		
Understands same/different	0.58	0.57
Understands on/under	0.66	1.00
Uses 3-word sentences	0.74	0.81
Uses words 75% understood	0.72	0.76
Can tell stories	0.75	0.83

Latent Transition Analysis

As mentioned previously, in many research scenarios involving young children, the focus is on longitudinal data (Duchnowski et al., 2013; Remmers et al., 2014; Suades-Gonzales et al., 2019). When the researcher would like to identify unknown subgroups in the population based upon measurements made at multiple points in time, LTA may be a very useful statistical technique. In addition to the probability of group membership at each point in time, as with LCA, LTA also provides the researcher with transition probabilities, which reflect the likelihood of individuals being in class c at time t being in class c^* at time $t+1$. For our example, this would take the form of the probability that a child who was in the "meets three developmental milestones" group at Time 1 moves into the "meets all developmental milestones" at Time 2. LTA can be used in any situation involving the same measurements being made at two or more points in time for the same sample of individuals and where the researcher is interested in learning whether there are unobserved subgroups in the population, based on the measures.

As we discussed previously, researchers using LCA typically focus on the probability of group membership and group differences in scores for the observed variables. These statistics are also important when researchers use LTA. In addition, the likelihood of individuals transitioning from a given subgroup at Time 1 to a given subgroup at Time 2 (transition probabilities) are also of interest to researchers using LTA. With a four-group LTA solution, these transition probabilities are written as

$$\pi_{ikm} = P(C_{it} = k | C_{it}-1 = m) = \frac{e^{(\alpha_k + \beta_k d_{i1} + \beta_{2k} d_{i2} + \beta_{3k} d_{i3})}}{\sum_{(q=1)}^{4} e^{(\alpha_q + \beta_{1q} d_{i1} + \beta_{2q} d_{i2} + \beta_{3q} d_{i3})}} \qquad (2)$$

Where

$\pi_{ikm} = P(C_{it} = k | C_{it}-1 = m) =$ Probability that an individual is in latent class k at time t, given that they were in latent class m at time t-1

Latent Transition Analysis

β_k = Odds of being in latent class k at Time 2 given being in latent class m at Time 1

a_k Intercept for regression model relating latent class membership at time 2 given latent class 1 membership

We can think of the LTA as a logistic regression model in which latent class membership at a later time is predicted by latent class membership at the previous time, as can be seen in Figure 2. This model produces unique transition probabilities for each pair of latent classes across adjacent time points. For example, in a-two-time points case with three classes at each time, the following transitions and associated probabilities are possible:

C1->C1

C1->C2

C1->C3

C2->C1

C2->C2

C2->C3

C3->C1

C3->C2

C3->C3.

As will be demonstrated below, these probabilities are useful for understanding developmental change over time by characterizing the most likely paths of changing group membership. Finally, it is important to note that while the measurements and sample need to be the same at each time point, there is no requirement that the latent classes are the same in either number or composition. In addition, not all possible transitions need to occur in an LTA. In other words, there may be some combinations of class memberships across time that simply don't occur.

Basic LTA Example

Given this background, let's now apply LTA to the developmental milestones data that we have been working with. LTA is carried out in the following steps:
1. Determine the classes at each time point independently.
2. Investigate whether the classes are the same across time periods (measurement invariance).
3. Estimate transition probabilities linking classes in adjacent time points.
4. Determine whether there is a trait component that partially explains the observed variables above and beyond the latent classes (random intercept LTA).
5. Measure relationships between covariates and latent class membership.

Determine the number of latent classes at each time point

In the prior section, we determined that at Time 1 there were 3 latent classes present in the data. We can also use LCA to investigate the latent class structure for Time 2. The fit indices and bootstrap LRT results for Time 2 appear in the bottom panel of Table 1. The AIC, BIC, and aBIC values were smallest for 3 classes suggesting that it is the optimal solution. In addition, the LRT hypothesis test for the 4-class solution was not statistically significant, indicating that it did not provide better fit to the data than did the 3-class model. Given these results, coupled with those from the LCA for Time 1, we conclude that the 3-class solution is optimal for both time points.

The probabilities for individuals in each class meeting the developmental milestones for the LCA results at Time 2 appear in Table 2. The pattern of these probabilities was similar to those for the Time 1 result. Specifically, there was a class of individuals who were likely to reach all 5 milestones, a second class whose members were likely to reach the milestones for using 3-word sentences, using

Latent Transition Analysis

words that 75% of non-family members can understand, and telling stories, and a third class of children who were not likely to meet any of the developmental milestones. Although the milestone specific probabilities were not the same across time, the patterns for the 3 classes at Time 2 were similar to those for the Time 1 classes.

Figure 2
Probability that developmental milestone reached by latent class for Times 1 and 2

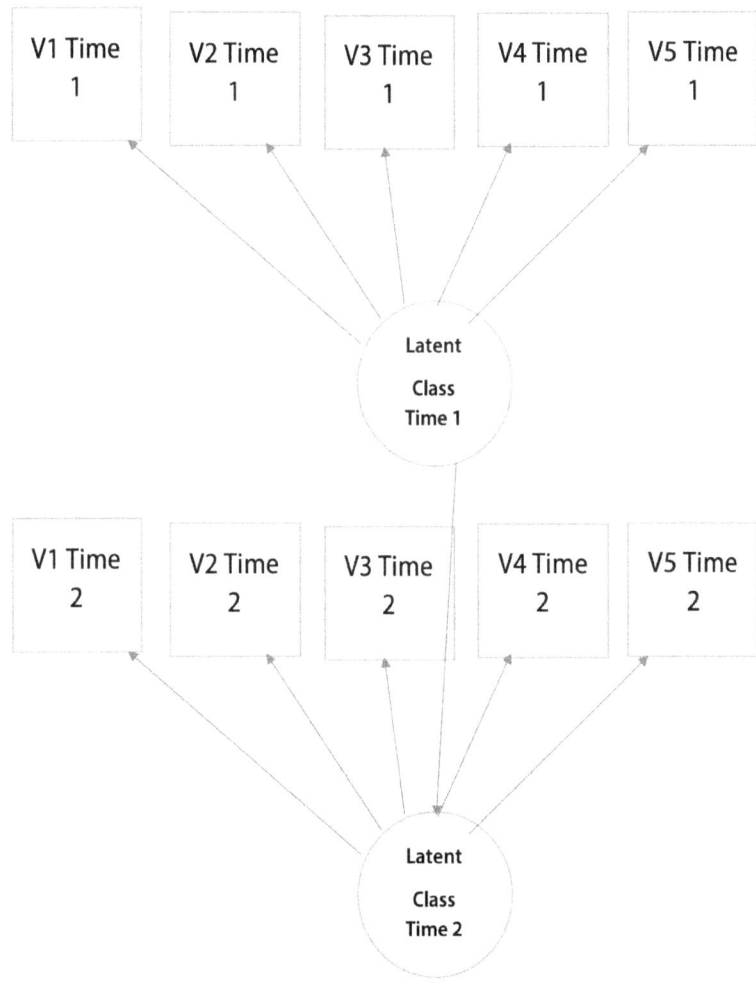

Investigate measurement invariance

In order to determine whether the LCA results for Times 1 and 2 are statistically equivalent (i.e., the latent classes at the two time points carry the same meaning with respect to the achievement of developmental milestones), we will compare the fit of two versions of the LTA. In the first version, we force the probabilities of achieving the milestones for each outcome variable to be the same in Times 1 and 2. This is called the invariant model. We then fit a second (non-invariant) model in which the milestone achievement probabilities are allowed to be different across the times. Finally, we compare the statistical fit of the invariant and non-invariant models by using the difference in their Chi-square fit statistics. An Excel spreadsheet that demonstrates this calculation is available for readers to access and use at https://holmesfinch.substack.com. The p-value for the invariance test was 0.20, which is not less than 0.05. Therefore, we conclude that the invariant and non-invariant models provide the same fit to the data, meaning that we can assume the milestone achievement probabilities are not different across time for the corresponding latent classes.

Estimate transition probabilities

Now that we have identified the latent classes at the two time points and have determined that they are not statistically different from one another, we are ready to fit the LTA model and obtain the transition probabilities. These values appear in Table 3. The rows represent latent class membership at Time 1 and the columns class membership at Time 2. From this table, we see that there is a probability of 0.71 that individuals who achieved all of the milestones at Time 1 would also achieve all milestones at Time 2. Furthermore, the probability of individuals in the "all milestones" group at Time 1 being in the "word use/stories" class at Time 2 was

Latent Transition Analysis

0.26, whereas the probability of going from the "all milestones" to the "no milestones" group was 0.03. We can use the same process to characterize transitions from the other two groups at Time 1. It appears that children in the "three milestones" class at Time 1 were most likely to transition to the "no milestones group" at Time 2, and least likely to remain in the three milestones class. Finally, individuals in the "no milestones" class at Time 1 were most likely to remain in that class at Time 2 and least likely to achieve all of the milestones.

Table 3
Transition probabilities for latent classes in Time 1 to latent classes in Time 2

Time 1	Time 2		
	1 (All)	2 (Word use/stories)	3 (None)
1 (All)	0.71	0.26	0.03
2 (Word use/stories)	0.25	0.18	0.58
3 (None)	0.09	0.33	0.58

Table 4
Frequencies (proportions) for each combination of latent classes

Class Time 1	Class Time 2	Frequency	Proportion
All	All	105	0.21
All	Word use/stories	39	0.08
All	None	5	0.01
Word use/stories	All	31	0.06
Word use/stories	Word use/stories	22	0.04
Word use/stories	None	73	0.15
None	All	20	0.04
None	Word use/stories	75	0.15
None	None	132	0.26

In addition to the transition probabilities, it is of interest to examine each combination of the latent class frequencies and proportions across the time periods. These values appear in Table 4. The largest group was those achieving none of the goals at either time, followed by those achieving all milestones at both points in time. The smallest group consisted of those who achieved all milestones at Time 1 and none at Time 2. Approximately equal numbers of children transitioned from the "no milestones" to the "word use/stories" group as went from the "word use/stories" class to the "no milestones" class. Finally, based upon these results it appears to be unlikely that a child would move from attaining none of the developmental milestones to then reaching all of them 6 months later.

Investigate trait component (Random intercept LTA)

A recent innovation in LTA has been the introduction of a latent variable, or factor, that helps to explain performance on the observed variables (e.g., developmental milestones) above and beyond that associated with the latent classes. This additional variable, labeled F in Figure 3, provides information about the observed variables that is not related to the temporal shifts modeled by the LTA. This random intercept LTA (RI-LTA) model can therefore be used to gain insights into both state (latent classes at multiple time points) and trait (time invariant factor) aspects of the observed variables. In the current example, the state specific performance on the developmental milestones is captured by the two latent classes and the transition probabilities linking them. The trait level information, which is captured by F, reflects performance on the milestones that is not developmental in nature, but rather specific to the individual across time.

Determining whether the RI-LTA model is more appropriate than the simple LTA approach is made by comparing the statistical fit of the two models using a difference in the chi-square goodness of fit values (likelihood ratio test) and the information indices

Figure 3
Transition probabilities for latent classes in Time 1 to latent classes in Time 2 Random intercept latent transition model with 5 observed variables measured at 2 time points

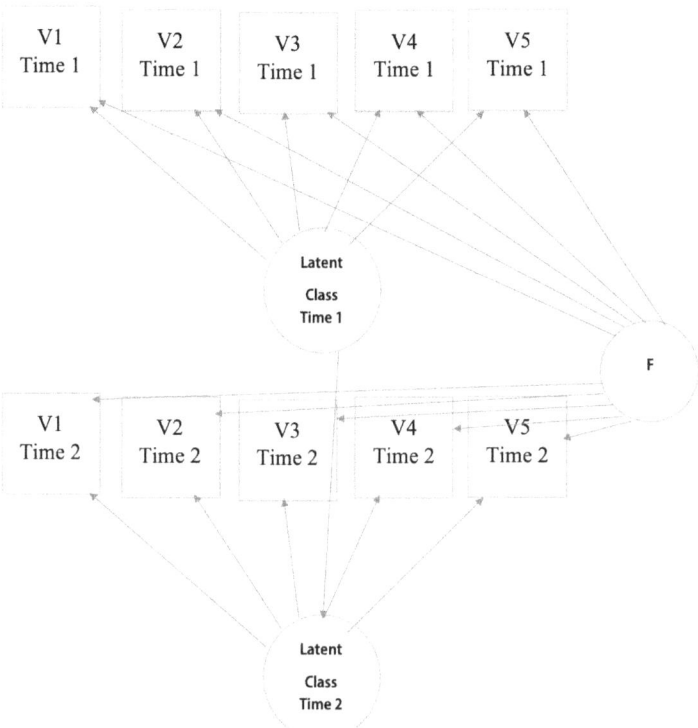

(AIC, BIC, aBIC), much as with comparing the invariant and non-invariant models. The results of this comparison appear in Table 5. The *p*-value for the likelihood ratio test (LRT) was 0.93, indicating that the statistical fit of the LTA and RI-LTA models was not different. Furthermore, the AIC, BIC, and aBIC values were all lower for the LTA model. Taken together, these results suggest that we do not need to retain the RI-LTA model. From a practical perspective, this means that there is no variability in the developmental milestones that is not captured by the temporal portion of the model (latent classes at Times 1 and 2 and the transition probabilities linking the two); i.e., no trait variability.

Incorporate covariate into LTA model

A final extension of the LTA model that can be quite useful in practice involves incorporating covariates as predictors of the individual latent classes as well as the transition probabilities. In this example, the covariate is the amount of time that parents report reading with their children every day. Covariates can be included in one of three ways. First, the covariate could only be associated with the first latent class variable, as in Figure 4. This model indicates that scores on the covariate are associated with membership in the latent class at Time 1 only. In the context of our example, this model would

Figure 4
Latent transition model with 5 observed variables measured at 2 time points and covariate related to latent class at time 1

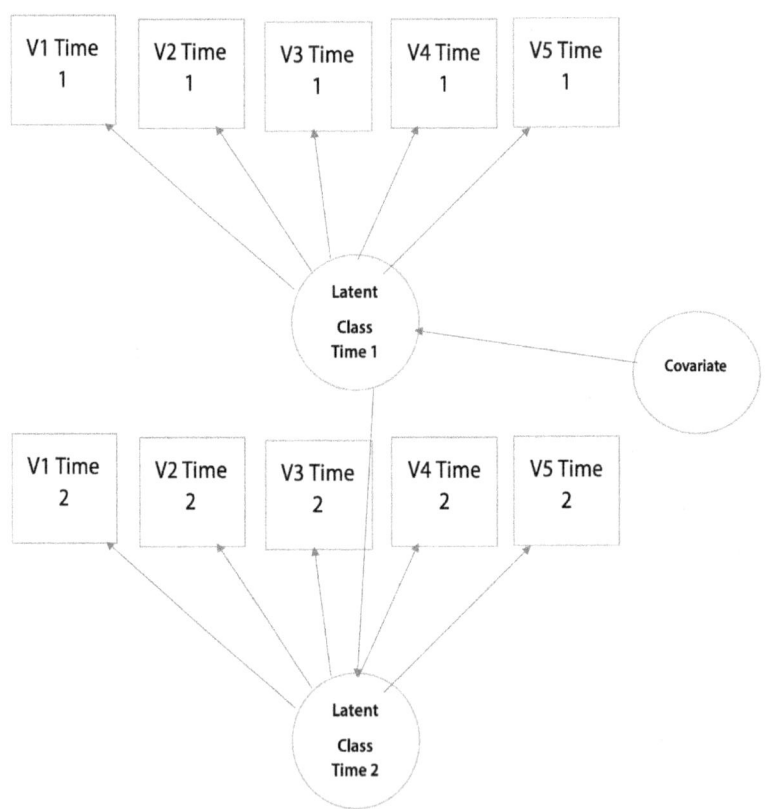

Latent Transition Analysis

indicate that the time parents spend reading to their children would not impact achievement of the developmental milestones after the first measures were made. The covariate can also be associated with the latent class membership at each time (Figure 5), meaning that time spent reading with children will affect the likelihood of achieving the milestones at both Times 1 and 2. Finally, the covariate can be a predictor of the latent classes at both times, as well as of the transition probabilities linking the two classes (Figure 6). This last relationship is essentially equivalent to an interaction between the covariate and the first latent class. In other words, if the covariate is significantly related to the transition probabilities from class membership at Time 1 to class membership at Time 2, we have an interaction

Figure 5
Latent transition model with 5 observed variables measured at 2 time points and covariate related to latent class at Times 1 and 2

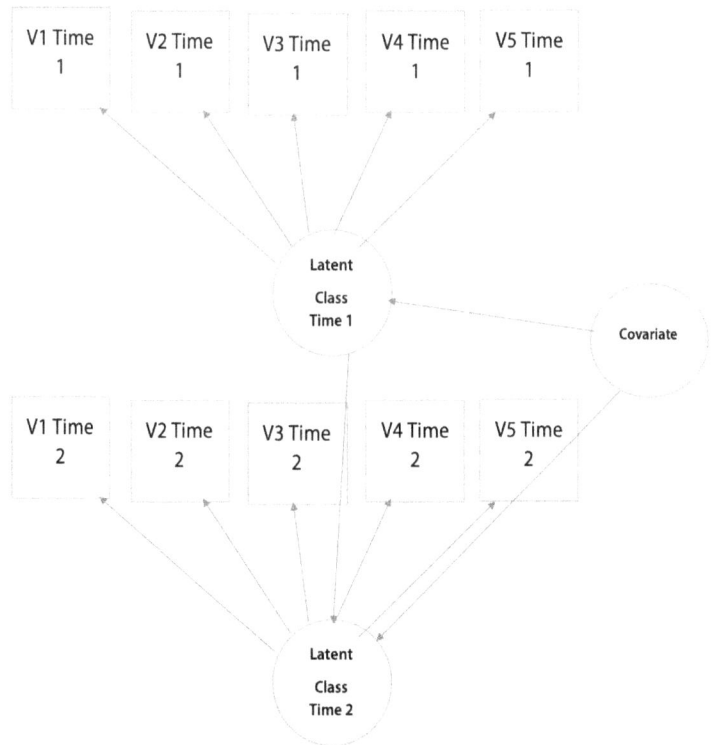

between the covariate and Time 1 latent class membership when predicting Time 2 latent class membership. For our example, such an interaction would mean that the amount of time parents spent reading to their children impacts membership in the latent classes at each time point, as well as the likelihood of progressing from one class to another between the times.

Figure 6
Latent transition model with 5 observed variables measured at 2 time points and covariate related to latent class at Times 1 and 2

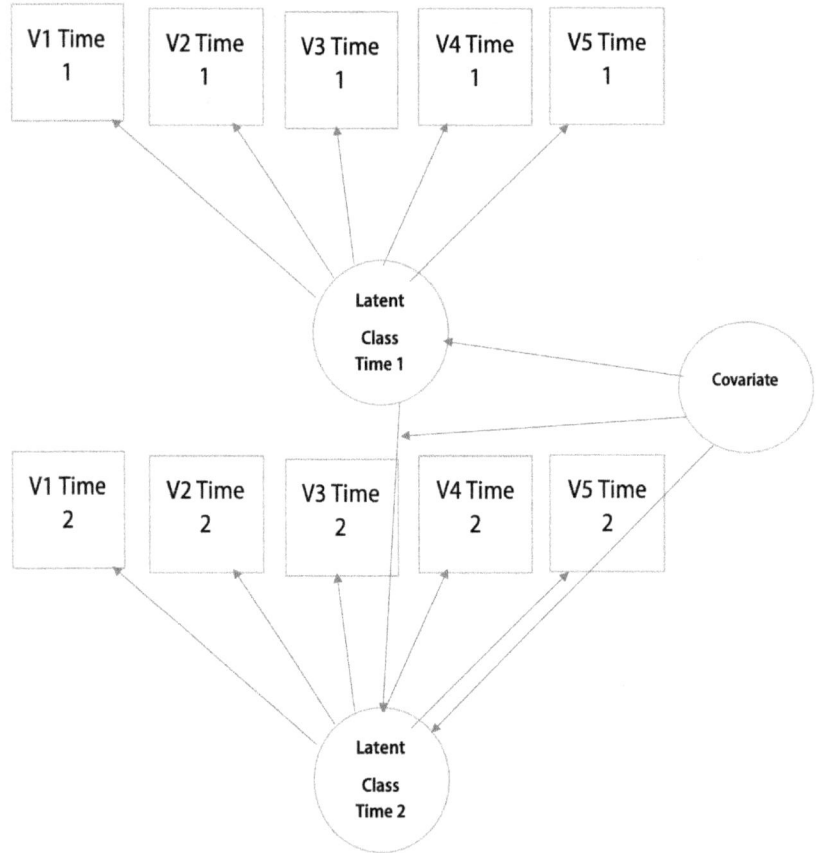

Table 5 includes statistics comparing fit of the LTA model including covariates with the basic LTA model. From these results, we would determine that the best fitting model includes a covariate related to latent classes at both time points as well as the transition probabilities. We reach this conclusion because this model yielded statistically significantly better fit than the others, based on the LRT p-value, and it had the lowest AIC, BIC, and aBIC values. Thus, further interpretation of the covariate will focus on the results from this model.

Table 5
Latent class analysis fit statistics for Times 1 and 2

Model	AIC	BIC	aBIC	BLRT p-value
LTA	6582.88	6679.81	6606.81	
RI-LTA	6591.95	6709.96	6621.09	0.93[1]
LTA with covariate on Time 1	6477.69	6583.06	6503.71	<0.001[1]
LTA with covariate on Times 1 and 2	6466.37	6580.16	6494.46	0.003[2]
LTA with covariate influencing transition probabilities	6456.81	6587.47	6489.07	<0.001[3] <0.001[3]

Note: [1]Versus LTA model; [2]Versus LTA model with covariate on Time 1; [3]Versus LTA model with covariate on Times 1 and 2

Table 6 includes the coefficients relating the covariate to the latent class variables at Times 1 and 2. For both time points, latent class 3 (unlikely to reach any of the milestones) is the reference category. This means that the coefficients in Table 6 reflect the impact of the covariate on the likelihood that a child is in either class 1 or 2 versus being in class 3. For example, at Time 1 the time spent reading was statistically significantly related to the coefficient for latent class 1 versus 3. The positive coefficient (2.70) means that children whose parents spent more time reading to them were more likely to be in latent class 1 (reaching all milestones) than in latent class 3 (reaching none of the milestones). Parental reading time was not significantly related to membership in latent class 2 (reaching some of the milestones) versus class 3. A similar pattern was evident at Time 2.

The relationship between reading time and the transition probabilities appear in Table 7. Three values of reading time per day were selected for examination, representing the mean value (2 hours), 1 standard deviation below the mean (1 hour) and 1 standard deviation above the mean (3 hours). The probability of switching classes from Times 1 to 2 was lowest for children whose parents read to them 1 hour per day. We reach this conclusion because the values on the diagonal of this portion of the table were larger than the diagonals for the other reading times. In addition, when children in the 1 hour reading group switched categories from the "three milestones" group, they were most likely to move into the "no milestones" group. Conversely, children in the "word use/stories" group whose parents read to them 3 hours per day were most likely to move into the "all milestones" group. Similarly, children in the "no milestones" class at Time 1 were most likely to move into the "word use/stories" class in Time 2. In summary, when parents reported reading with their child 3 hours per day, the child was most likely to move into the adjacent higher category, or to remain in the highest category. In contrast, when parents read to their children 1 hour per day, they were unlikely to change class, or to move into the adjacent lower class in the case of the word use/stories group.

Table 7
Transition probabilities at different levels of the covariate

Relationship	C1 vs C3, Time 1	C2 vs C3, Time 1	C1 vs C3, Time 2	C2 vs C3, Time 2
Time reading per day on Times 1 and 2	2.70*	0.60	3.58*	0.53

Reading Time = 1 hour

Time 1	Time 2		
	1 (All)	2 (Word use/stories)	3 (None)
1 (All)	0.94	0.06	0.00
2 (Word use/stories)	0.07	0.47	0.46
3 (None)	0.10	0.11	0.79

Reading Time = 2 hours

Time 1	Time 2		
	1 (All)	2 (Word use/stories)	3 (None)
1 (All)	0.55	0.38	0.06
2 (Word use/stories)	0.06	0.38	0.55
3 (None)	0.10	0.37	0.53

Reading Time = 3 hours

Time 1	Time 2		
	1 (All)	2 (Word use/stories)	3 (None)
1 (All)	0.69	0.30	0.01
2 (Word use/stories)	0.63	0.31	0.03
3 (None)	0.06	0.70	0.23

Discussion

Research focused on young children often involves longitudinal data in which measurements are made on the same individuals at multiple points in time (Duchnowski et al., 2013; Remmer et al., 2014; Suades-Gonzales et al., 2019). In some of these scenarios, researchers are particularly interested in identifying underlying subgroups within the data at each time point, based upon a set of measured variables. The purpose of this paper was to demonstrate LTA, which allows for the investigation of such subgroups as well as an estimation of the relationships between them in the form of transition probabilities. In addition, LTA can also be used to investigate relationships between additional covariates and latent class membership, as well as the transition probabilities themselves. Finally, we saw that LTA models can also incorporate a random intercept, which allows for investigation of trait specific effects on the observed variables that are invariant across time.

Although it is certainly a useful tool, LTA does have limitations that need to be considered by researchers using it. First, when the latent classes in the different time periods are not invariant, interpretation of the results is not as straightforward as was highlighted in this paper. Certainly, LTA remains a useful tool in such cases, but when the direct correspondence between classes across time does not exist, researchers will need to devote greater attention to understanding the implications of the transition probabilities and movement from one group to another. Second, LTA requires relatively larger samples than is the case for many other statistical analyses (Nylund-Gibson, et al., 2023). Recommendations for a minimum sample size are between 300 and 500 (Nylund-Gibson & Choi, 2018; Finch & Bronk, 2011), with agreement that larger samples will yield more stable results. Another issue to consider when working with LTA is the invariance of the latent classes and transition probabilities across known groups in the population, such as treatment and control groups, different grade levels, etc. Researchers who believe that changes over time in the measured variables might be associated with such a grouping variable should investigate whether this is indeed the case, using an invariance approach similar to how we investigated invariance across time points (see Schmiege et al., 2018).

LTA can be carried out using a variety of software packages, most notably Latent Gold or Mplus. Analysis for the current example was done using Mplus, version 8.6. The programs and data are available for the interested reader at https://holmesfinch.substack.com/. As of this writing (October 2023), the freely available open sourced R software package does not feature a fully functioning library for fitting a complete LTA model, such as the one demonstrated here. In addition, the reader interested in learning more about the practice of using LTA and current issues around it is encouraged to read Nylund-Gibson et al. (2023).

Impact statement

This manuscript describes a statistical approach to modeling change over time that can be characterized in terms of population subgroups. This approach can be very useful to researchers in early childhood, who often work with longitudinal data in which change is common and of interest.

References

American Academy of Pediatrics. (2019). *Caring for Your baby and young child: Birth to age 5 (7th Ed)*. https://doi.org/10.1542/9781610023443

Bauer, D. J., & Curran, P. J. (2004). The integration of continuous and discrete latent variable models: Potential problems and promising opportunities. *Psychological Methods, 9*(1), 3-29. https://doi.org/10.1037/1082-989X.9.1.3

Bosnic, I., Ciccozzi, F., Crnkovic, I., Cavrak, I., Di Nitto, E., Mirandola, R., & Zagar, M. (2019). Managing diversity in distributed software development education-A longitudinal case study. *ACM Transactions on Computing Education, 19*(2), -23. https://doi.org/10.1145/3218310

Collins, L. M., & Lanza, S. T. (2010). *Latent class and latent transition analysis*. John Wiley & Sons, Inc. https://doi.org/10.1002/9780470567333

Duchnowski, A. J., Kutash, K., Green, A. L., Ferron, J. M., Wagner, M., & Vengrofski, B. (2013). Parent support services for families of children with emotional disturbances served in elementary school special education settings: Examination of data from the Special Education Elementary Longitudinal Study. *Journal of Disability Policy Studies, 24*(1), 36–52. https://doi.org/10.1177/10442073124608

Finch, W. H., & Bronk, K. C. (2011). Conducting confirmatory latent class analysis using Mplus. *Structural Equation Modeling, 18*(1), 132–151. https://doi.org/10.1080/10705511.2011.532732

Goodman, L. A. (2002). Latent class analysis: The empirical study of latent types, latent variables, and latent structures. In J. A. Hagenaars & A. L. McCutcheon (Eds.), *Applied latent class analysis*. Cambridge University. doi:10.1017/CBO9780511499531.002

Lazarsfeld, P. F., & Henry, N. W. (1968). *Latent structure analysis*. Houghton Mifflin. https://doi.org/10.4236/jbm.2020.811009

McLachlan, G., & Peel, D. (2000). *Finite mixture models*. John Wiley & Sons, Inc. https://doi.org/10.1002/0471721182

Muthèn, L. K., & Muthèn, B. O. (2022). *Mplus, user's guide (8th Ed.)*. Muthèn and Muthèn.

Nylund-Gibson, K., Garber, A. C., Carter, D. B., Chan, M., & Arch, D. A. N. (2023). Ten frequently asked questions about latent transition analysis. *Psychological Methods, 28*(2), 284–300. https://doi.org/10.1037/met0000486

Nylund-Gibson, K. L., & Choi, A. Y. (2018). Ten frequently asked questions about latent class analysis. *Translational Issues in Psychological Science, 4*(4), 440–461. https://doi.org/10.1037/tps0000176

Nylund, K. L., Asparouhov, T., & Muthén, B. O. (2007). Deciding on the number of classes in latent class analysis and growth mixture modeling: A Monte Carlo simulation study. *Structural Equation Modeling, 14*(4), 535–569. https://doi.org/10.1080/10705510701575396

Remmers, T., Broeren, S. M. L., Renders, C. M., Hirasing, R. A., van Grieken, A., & Raat, H. (2014). A longitudinal study of children's outside play using family environment and perceived physical environment as predictors. *International Journal of Behavioral Nutrition and Physical Activity, 11*, 1–9. https://doi.org/10.1186/1479-5868-11-76

Schmiege, S.J., Masyn, K.E., & Bryan, A.D. (2018). Confirmatory latent class analysis: Illustrations of empirically driven and theoretically driven model constraints. *Organizational Research Methods, 21*(4), 983–1001.

Suades-Gonzalez, E., Forns, J., Garcia-Esteban, R., Lopez-Vicente, M., Esanola, M., Alvarez-Pedrero, M., Julvez, J., Caceres, A., Basagana, X., Lopez-Sala, A., & Sunyer, J. (2017). A longitudinal study on attention development in primary school children with and without teacher-reported symptoms of ADHD. *Frontiers in Developmental Psychology, 8*, 1–10. https://doi.org/10.3389/fpsyg.2017.00655

List of Contibutors

W. Holmes Finch is the George and Frances Ball Professor of Educational Psychology at Ball State University where he teaches statistics and measurement. He conducts research in latent variable modeling, multivariate statistics, and robust methods. He also enjoys collaborating with researchers in the social and health sciences.

Brian F. French is a Regents Professor and director of the Learning and Performance Research Center at Washington State University. His research focuses on educational and psychological measurement issues, with the goal of addressing fairness issues in decisions made about individuals. Dr. French teaches courses in measurement/psychometrics, statistics, research methods, and quantitative methods. He is active in national service, involved in technical advisory committee, and is the editor of the Measurement, Statistics, and Research Design section of the Journal of Experimental Education.

Brittany Garza is a School Psychology doctoral student at the University of Southern Mississippi and is a Board Certified Behavior Analyst (BCBA) with experience in public school and clinic settings. Brittany holds a Master of Education in Curriculum and Instruction, Teaching and Learning, with a focus on autism spectrum disorders from Arizona State University. Prior to her master's degree, she earned a Bachelor of Fine Arts from the University of Arizona. Brittany's research interests include teaching behavioral skills to prevent emergent challenging behavior and effective class-wide strategies for neurodiverse learners. Brittany is specifically interested in evaluating feasible and effective class-wide strategies for inclusive classrooms.

Abigail Lawson is enrolled in a School Psychology doctoral program at the University of Southern Mississippi. Abigail holds a Master of Arts in Psychology and received her Bachelors of Science in Psychology from Mississippi State University. She has experience working with children diagnosed with autism spectrum disorder and providing school consultation with teachers and school administrators. Abigail's research interest include Tier I and Tier II supports and intervention within the Positive Behavior Intervention and Supports framework. Specifically, she is interested in educating and training teachers on feasible interventions to increase academically engaged behaviors at a class-wide and individual level.

Zachary LaBrot, Ph.D., is an Assistant Professor of School Psychology at the University of Southern Mississippi. Dr. LaBrot's research interests include consultation in early childhood education settings, class wide interventions, and behavioral parent training. Additionally, Dr. LaBrot is a proudly practicing licensed psychologist.

Emily Maxime is a fourth-year graduate student in the University of Southern Mississippi's School Psychology Doctoral Program. Emily's research interests examine the implementation of intervention and consultation strategies that can be generalized by students and teachers to help further their overall success at school and home.

Tyler Smith, Ph.D., is an Assistant Professor of School Psychology in the Department of Educational, School, and Counseling Psychology at the University of Missouri. Dr. Smith's research focuses on family engagement in education, school-based consultation, and systematic review/meta-analyses.

Perspectives on Early Childhood Psychology and Education

PECPE publishes twice a year, in the fall and spring. These two issues on specific focuses are typically guest-edited and can also include a few general articles.

Editorial Policy and Submission Guidelines

Perspectives on Early Childhood Psychology and Education focuses on publishing original contributions from a broad range of psychological and educational perspectives relevant to infants, young children (to age 8 years), families, and caregivers. Manuscripts incorporating evidence-based research, theory, and practice within clinical, community, developmental, neurological, and school psychology perspectives are considered. In addition, the journal accepts test and book reviews, literature reviews, program descriptions and evaluations, clinical studies, and other professional materials of interest to psychologists and educators working with young children. Proposals for special focus topics may be made to the Editor.

Format: Manuscripts should be original work not currently submitted for publication to other journals. Authors must follow the guidelines of the Publication Manual of the American Psychological Association (Sixth Edition). Manuscripts may not exceed 35 double-spaced pages in length, including the cover page, abstract, references, tables, and figures.

Submission: Submit an electronic copy of the manuscript for editorial review. Avoid including any identifying author information in the text. Selection of manuscripts is based on blind peer review. Include a cover page with the following information: the title of article, author(s) full name(s), title(s), institution or professional affiliations, and mailing and email address of primary author. The cover page will not be sent to reviewers.

Selection Criteria:
- Importance of topic in early childhood psychology and education
- Theory and research related to content
- Contribution to professional practice in early childhood psychology and education
- Clear and concise writing
- Submit manuscripts to the Editor electronically at the following email address: PECPE@bsu.edu.

Volume 8, Issue 2 of
Perspectives on Early Childhood Psychology and Education
was published in Fall 2023
by Pace University Press

Cover and interior layout by Kayleigh Woltal
The journal was typeset in Minion and Myriad
and printed by Lightning Source

Pace University Press

Director: Manuela Soares
Faculty Advisor: Eileen Kreit
Design Consultant: Joseph Caserto
Production Associate: Lucely Garcia

Graduate Assistants: Erin Hurley and Kayleigh Woltal
Graduate Student Aide: Elizabeth Abrams

www.ingramcontent.com/pod-product-compliance
Lightning Source LLC
Chambersburg PA
CBHW061450300426
44114CB00014B/1918